Federal Public Policy
on Aging since 1960

FEDERAL PUBLIC POLICY ON AGING SINCE 1960

An Annotated Bibliography

Compiled by William E. Oriol

Bibliographies and Indexes in Gerontology, Number 5

Greenwood Press
New York • Westport, Connecticut • London

Library of Congress Cataloging-in-Publication Data

Federal public policy on aging since 1960.

  (Bibliographies and indexes in gerontology,
ISSN 0743-7560 ; no. 5)
  Bibliography: p.
  Includes index.
  1. Aged—Government policy—United States—
Bibliography. I. Oriol, William E. II. Series.
Z7164.04F43 1987 [HQ1064.U5]   016.3626   87-8343
ISBN 0-313-25286-6 (lib. bdg. : alk. paper)

Library of Congress Catalog Card Number: 87-8343
ISBN: 0-313-25286-6
ISSN: 0743-7560

First published in 1987

Greenwood Press, Inc.
88 Post Road West, Westport, Connecticut 06881

Printed in the United States of America

The paper used in this book complies with the
Permanent Paper Standard issued by the National
Information Standards Organization (Z39.48-1984).

10 9 8 7 6 5 4 3 2 1

To Patricia Glidden Oriol
Wife, Partner, Friend

CONTENTS

viii   Contents

FOREWORD

The annotated bibliographies in the Greenwood Press series, Bibliographies and Indexes in Gerontology, provide answers to the fundamental question, "What is known?" Their purpose is simple, yet profound: to provide comprehensive reviews and references for the work done in various fields of gerontology. They are based on the fact that it is no longer possible for anyone to comprehend the vast body of research and writing in even one sub-speciality without years of work.

This fact has become true only in recent years. When I was an undergraduate at Duke University (Class of '52) I think no one at Duke had even heard of gerontology, there were no courses offered on the subject, and almost no one in the world was identified as a gerontologist. Now there are more than five thousand professional members of the Gerontological Society of America, and thousands of courses in gerontology are being offered by most major and many minor colleges and universities. When I was an undergraduate there was only one gerontological publication in existence, the Journal of Gerontology, begun in 1945. Now there are a dozen professional journals and several dozen books in gerontology published each year.

The reasons for this substantial growth are well-known: the dramatic increase in the number of aged in the United States, the shift from family to public responsibility for the security and care of the elderly, the recognition of aging as a social problem, and the growth of science in general. It is less well-known that this explosive growth in interest and knowledge has been accompanied by the demand for new solutions to the old problem of comprehending and "keeping up on" current research within a field of knowledge. The old indexes and library card catalogues are becoming increasingly inadequate for the job. On-line computer indexes and abstracts are one solution but make no evaluative selections nor organize sources as logically as possible with these more widely available annotated bibliographies.

These bibliographies will obviously be useful for researchers who need to know what research has (or has not) been done in their field. The annotations usually contain enough information so that the researcher does not have to search out the original articles. In the past, the "review of literature" has often been haphazard and rarely comprehensive because of the large investment of time and money that would be required by a truly comprehensive review. Now, using these bibliographies, researchers can be more confident that they are not missing important previous research or duplicating past efforts and "reinventing the wheel." It may well become a standard and expected practice for researchers to consult such bibliographies, even before they start their research.

These bibliographies will also be useful reference tools for teachers, students, policy analysts, lawyers, legislators, administrators, and any intelligent person who wishes to find out what is known about a given topic in gerontology.

Public policy on aging is clearly one of the most important topics in gerontology, perhaps the most important topic in applied gerontology, because public policy determines the setting and most of the attempted solutions to the numerous problems of aging. Until the findings of gerontology are incoporated into public policy any benefits of the scientific work are likely to be scattered and meager.

Furthermore, public policy has been growing in importance because there is a growing consensus that many (if not most) of the problems of aging are caused by social and economic systems of aging, and could be ameliorated or possibly solved by public programs. This has led to the well-known mushrooming of public programs for the aged, which have resulted in more money being spent by the federal government on the elderly (28% of the budget in 1985) than on any other category of expenditures, including national defense.

Within the general field of public policy, federal policy is clearly the most important. State and local policies are also important, especially on a regional level, but federal policy usually sets the context and often provides the major funding for local programs in aging.

Thus, this bibliography is a major information resource for all planners, administrators, practitioners, and others involved with the elderly, as well as for academicians and students interested in applied gerontology.

The author of this bibliography has done an outstanding job of covering all of the relevant information and organizing it into an easily accessible form. Not only are there 751 annotated references organized into 35 sections, but there is also an appendix on congressional committees and national organizations as further sources of information, an author index, and a comprehensive subject index with several cross-references for each item in the bibliography. Thus, relevant material in this volume can be searched for in several ways: 1) looking up a given subject in the subject index; 2) looking up a given author in the author index; 3) turning to the section in Part Two that covers the topic; or 4) looking over the references in Part One for general critiques and overviews.

William Oriol is an unusually qualified expert in the area of federal public policy because of his sixteen years on the staff of the United States Senate Special Committee on Aging (including twelve years as its staff director). It can safely be said that there were no important issues concerning federal public policy that were not dealt with by this committee during those years. Furthermore, Oriol has remained an active and productive gerontologist during the years since then.

So it is with great pleasure that we add this bibliography to this series. I believe this volume will be found to be the most useful, comprehensive, and easily accessible reference work in its field. I will appreciate any comments you care to send to me.

Erdman B. Palmore
Center for the Study of Aging and Human Development
Box 3003, Duke University Medical Center
Durham, NC 27710

PREFACE

A bibliography on public policy on aging not only must deal with official actions taken by the government, but also with the issues that cause such actions to be taken or, at least, proposed.

The amount of material that has been written dealing with these causes and effects of public policy on aging is staggering; listing it all in this bibliography would have been impossible. However, by carefully choosing the representative literature to be included, a balance was achieved that reflects all of the literature available concerning both official government action and any underlying issues. This selection process did require difficult decisions. For example: How much weight should be given to early proposals that incisively explained problems in need of correction, but which later were superseded by other, quite different, policy decisions? How much attention should be given to individual issues, and how much to far-ranging analyses of public policy on aging in general? Was an excellent journal article that dealt only tangentially with policy--but which shed light on an intricate issue--to be superseded by a lesser article, but one that was more directly concerned with legislation or programs?

Such questions are intensified by the sheer complexity of aging as a social, political, economic, and personal force. When I served on the United States Senate Special Committee on Aging as a professional staff member from 1963 to 1967, and as staff director from 1967 to 1979, I frequently observed that almost any topic discussed in the daily newspapers could be related to aging. And, with a little more thought, to a legislative consideration. The challenge was to narrow down the number of topics to a manageable amount and then to select those with clear relevance to immediate or long-range potential action.

Similar challenges arose during the preparation of this bibliography. A few words, therefore, are provided here to help the reader/researcher understand the rationale for the organization of this volume's contents and the selection of the individual entries.

This bibliography covers a period beginning in 1960 and continuing through early 1986, dealing primarily with federal policy on aging but also taking note of several programs requiring federal-state action. Its entries reflect the beginnings in 1960 of the government's awareness that public support of national action on aging was mounting, not only for social insurance to cover hospital costs of older persons, but also on other aging-related matters of significant concern as well. A more contemporary wave of analyses is also thoroughly covered. For example, recent studies protest perceived inequities said to give advantage to the higher-income elderly while failing to meet the needs of the low-income seniors and the "old-old" who stand at a greater risk of developing a chronic illness requiring costly long-term care.

Part One, "Federal Aging Policy: General Critiques, Key Themes," contains 162 entries, with annotations dealing with book-length or other evaluations declaring the failure, partial success, or considerable achievement resulting from federal action that intended to make life better for our citizens in their later years.

In addition to global appraisals, Part One also offers entries dealing with key principles or conundrums in the making of federal policy on aging. Numerous references are made, pro and con, to age as the criterion for eligibility in certain programs, for example. Some items have been selected because they shed historical perspective on the development of policy. White House conferences and presidential messages are cited, largely because they provide means of comparing expressed aspirations with actual accomplishments. A number of entries related to legal issues are included to emphasize practical questions arising in the implementation of benefit or service programs.

Part Two, "Specific Programs and Issues," contains 589 entries and addresses topics of concern related to federal public policy on aging. The selection process was even more sternly applied than in Part One in order to provide some mention of the many policy strands that must be considered if an overall pattern is to be discerned. Therefore, though Part Two addresses far too many topics for exhaustive treatment of any of them, its entries provide the reader with an overview of programs and issues related to aging in the United States.

In giving great weight, for instance, to long term care and related topics, this bibliography concurs with judgments that chronic care/support needs now constitute the major challenge in aging and will become dramatically more challenging in the very near future. Caregiving is emphasized in the section on women, as it is in the entries included on family policy.

The policies, programs, and issues of aging are too often viewed separately without taking into account the linkages that exist among them. In order to reflect this interdependency, a considerable effort was made to provide a truly comprehensive subject index. Most entries have at least two cross-references; a substantial number have three or even four. Entries are listed alphabetically under each topic heading and a separate author index refers to all names given in each entry or in the annotation. Entry numbers are consecutive throughout Parts One and Two.

In assembling the entries, I had a headstart provided by my years with the United States Senate Special Committee on Aging, to which many authors frequently sent their work, along with their hopes that their messages would be heeded. The committee cast its own net for writings of all kinds, a process in which the Legislative Reference Service of the Library of Congress was remarkably helpful. Upon leaving the committee, I became familiar with a large number of the works represented in this bibliography because of my writings on varied subjects, all related to public policy.

To update and broaden my sources, I began with a thorough review of all articles that have appeared in The Gerontologist since it began publication in 1960, paying particular heed to references cited by each author. I then followed the same procedure with key books on aging policy and with other journals primarily or significantly focused on aging.

My base of research operations was the National Gerontology Resource Center at the Washington D.C. headquarters of the American Association of Retired Persons. Only rarely did their excellent collection lack a specific book or periodical. The Ollie A. Randall Library of The National Council on the Aging was also useful.

Advertisements and book reviews were scanned for current publications. Frequent inspections were regularly made of relevant sections of Nathan W. Shock's "List of Current Publications in Gerontology and Geriatrics," as published until 1980 in the Journal of Gerontology. Though designed for other purposes, The Aging and Social Welfare Annotated Bibliography Series, issued by the Gerontology Studies Program at the School of Social Welfare, University of California at Berkeley, was well worth inspecting for important works that had public policy content. I am grateful to the series editor, Mary O'Day, of Berkeley, for making the extensive compilation available to me. The National Council on the Aging's Current Literature in Aging was similarly useful.

An especially rich source, provided through the AARP National Gerontology Resource Center, resulted from a search by its AgeLine computerized bibliographic data base. My heartfelt thanks go to Center Director Paula M. Lovas for her generous interest and assistance, and to Center staff member Jo-Ellen Knoerl for her cooperation and ingenuity in making the best possible use of AgeLine. One of the most valuable outcomes of the AgeLine search was the identification of papers from journals outside the aging orbit, as well as a number of books that otherwise might have escaped detection.

For the formidable task of preparing a cross-referenced, camera-ready manuscript, I was once again affectionately awed by the skill and determination of my wife, Patricia Glidden Oriol. To this task, she devoted hours that are best left uncounted. I would also like to extend my appreciation to a distinguished gerontologist, Ethel Shanas, for valuable advice she provided at the very beginning of this task. My thanks go, too, to Erdman Palmore, advisor to Greenwood Press for this series of bibliographies. He helped me to envision the scope that this bibliography should have. Mary R. Sive, editor of Social and Behavioral Sciences for Greenwood Press, patiently provided guidance throughout.

Sorely tempted to make frequent references to the publications of the United States Senate Special Committee on Aging, the United States House of Representatives Select Committee on Aging, and other congressional units, I nevertheless exercised restraint and did not cite published hearings, even though many are worthy of note. By the entry of a fairly substantial number of congressional reports, primarily from the Senate and House Committees on Aging, I am hopeful that the careful researcher will be guided by the references within most such reports to individual hearings and witnesses. Note: See Appendix for additional commentary on congressional committees and national organizations as information sources.

There have been no easy answers to questions such as those posed in paragraph two of this preface. Entries were selected for widely varying reasons, many for their obvious relevance to policy, others because they made important points on matters that should be considered as policy is formulated. Demographic information, despite its importance as a factor in making policy, is not cited because it is more readily available in other formats. On the other hand, several entries are related to J.F. Fries' "compression of morbidity" thesis because of its public policy implications.

Because they are so numerous and may be found in conference collections, the voluminous background papers and reports prepared in advance of the 1961, 1971, and 1981 White House Conferences on Aging are not represented in this bibliography. Two preliminary papers for the 1961 White House Conference are included, however, because they express so aptly historically interesting and contrary viewpoints on the fundamental federal role. One was written by then New Jersey Governor Robert Meyner, who argued for greater national attention to aging; the other by Senator Barry Goldwater, who asked for strengthened reliance on family, private resources, and state and local government for action on aging.

All of the annotations are my personal summaries. By consistently questioning a number of personal attitudes and opinions while working on this bibliography, I believe I succeeded in remaining objective when writing each description. In some cases, I found reason to look for new answers or, at least, new questions. Paring the content of the annotations down to a minimum was sometimes painful, but I believe that each gives sufficient information about the usefulness of the work cited.

I hope that this bibliography will help others, in their search for data and ideas, to raise new questions of their own. Monumental changes in federal public policy in aging have occurred since 1960. The rate of change will probably accelerate. So must our thinking. So must our concern. So must our insistence that there be as many triumphs in aging as there are temporary difficulties.

PART ONE

FEDERAL AGING POLICY:
GENERAL CRITIQUES, KEY THEMES

FEDERAL AGING POLICY:

GENERAL CRITIQUES, KEY THEMES

001 Achenbaum, W.A. (1983). Shades of gray: Old age, American values, and Federal policies since 1920. Boston: Little, Brown & Co. 216p.
Asserts that elderly were among the last populations to be affected by the long-term process of modernization. Social Security underlying values are analyzed, as are "Great Society" policy dilemmas. The "Shocking Sobering Seventies" seen as triggering doubts about policy directions and purposes. Proposal is made for "double-decker social welfare program" using objective eligibility standards for essential needs, and age-specific programs where needed. Early Reagan years deemed inconclusive, but potential milestone.

002 Achenbaum, W.A. (1978). Old age in the new land: The American experience since 1790. Baltimore: Johns Hopkins University Press, 237p.
Informative, thoughtful historical perspective on interactions of public policy with changing societal appraisals of roles and status of older persons, including analysis of modernization impact. Social Security enactment in 1935 seen as a watershed action establishing the first nationwide structure for older Americans. Subsequent programs briefly described; persistence of discrimination probed. Numerous notes, strong on cultural/economic views.

003 Alexander, G.J. (1981). Age and the law. In: Johnston, P.W. (Ed.). Perspectives on aging: Exploding the myths. Cambridge MA., Ballinger Publishing Co., 45-69.
Subjects key Federal policies on aging to legal analysis and concludes that societal ambivalence about aging is reflected in laws and program. Questions adequacy of anti-discrimination statutes, health care limitations on autonomy, and paternal tendencies in guardianship laws. Useful references.

004 American Association of Retired Persons. (1971). The 1971 White House Conference on Aging: The end of a beginning? Washington DC: 85p.
A survey of actions in aging since the 1961 White House Conference on Aging, intended to "help sharpen the focus of the 1971 Conference." AARP consolidated more than 700 1961 recommendations into 160.

005 Atchley, R.C. (1985). Social forces and aging: An introduction to social gerontology. (Fourth Edition). Belmont CA: Wadsworth Publishing Co, 510p.
Serving its purpose as an introductory text, this volume also offers useful, succinct observations on Federal policy in Chapters 16-19. The author is skeptical of the ability of the market economy to meet certain housing, health care, and transportation needs. His commentary in government response to the aged in Chapter 17 is brief but incisive. Outstanding bibliography.

006   Atchley, R.C. (1978). Aging as a social problem: An overview. In: Seltzer, M.M.; Corbett, S.L.; Atchley,.R.C. (Eds.). Social problems of the aging: Readings. Belmont CA: Wadsworth Publishing Co. 4-22.
Brief descriptions of major Federal programs comprise a useful summary of society's responses to problems of older people. Lack of coordination among programs emphasized. Improved image of the elderly seen as changing future policy directions, but current severe problems must be addressed.

007   Austin, C.D.; Loeb, M.B. (1982). Why age is relevant in social policy and Practice. In: Neugarten, B.L. (Ed.). Age or need? Public policies for older people. Beverly Hills: Sage Publications, 263-288.
Predicts that chronological age will remain a major screening criterion in "a continuum of allocative principles" in the near term. Gradual inclusion of need-based and other criteria expected to bring incremental change, but the age factor remains "familiar, easy to understand, simple to determine, and politically useful for constituencies."

008   Baumhover, L.A.; Jones, J.D. (1977). Handbook of American aging programs. Westport CT: Greenwood Press, 188p.
A descriptive, rather than analytical, treatment of programs, offering basic information and advice on implementation in the community. Contributing authors deal with planning, direct services, volunteerism, and advocacy. Detailed reports on ombudsman programs in Michigan, South Carolina.

009   Binstock, R.H.; Levin, M.A.; Weatherly, R. (1985). Political dilemmas of social intervention. In: Binstock, R.H.; Shanas, E. (Eds.). Handbook of aging and the social sciences. New York: Van Nostrand Reinhold Company, 589-618.
Examines causes of political limitations on effective policy intervention, including legislative inhibitions, Executive Branch implementation strategies, fragmentation through Federalism and private sector participation, and a tendency to perpetuate programs. Many examples. A timely, frank account. Excellent references.

010   Binstock, R.H.; Shanas, E. (1985). Handbook of aging and the social sciences, Second Edition. New York: Van Nostrand Reinhold Company, 809p.
Social aspects of aging discussed through the systematic perspectives of a variety of social sciences in 26 chapters by eminent authors from all relevant disciplines. Historical perspectives provided. Many chapters have useful sections on policy implications. Scope and content are broader than in first edition.

011   Binstock, R.H. (1983). The aged as scapegoat. The Gerontologist, 23(2), 136-43.
Argues that an era of "compassionate stereotypes" portraying the elderly as generally poor and frail but nevertheless deserving of advocacy and Federal action has ended, to be replaced by a new set of erroneous axioms saying that the elderly have won unfair advantage in public policy. Suggests advocacy and policy shifts that would give more effective attention to elders most in need. Asks gerontologists to emphasize heterogeneity of older persons.

012   Binstock, R.H. (1980). There is an urgent need to confront basic issues. Generations, (Special Issue on Public Policy) 4(1), 6-8, 53.
Puts a minimum-but-adequate income for all older persons as primary policy goal,

on grounds that Social Security leaves millions of elderly in poverty, even with help from the Supplemental Security Income program. Other proposals: a reversal of biomedical research priorities to put priority attention on reduction and reversal of senility, and absorption of categorical aging services into a generic system.

013   Binstock, R.H. (1978). Federal policy toward the aging—its inadequacies and its politics. In: Hubbard, J.P. (Ed.). The economics of aging: The economic, political and social implications of growing old in America: Issues book, Washington DC: The National Journal, 57-64.
Finds that Federal expenditures on aging, approximately one-quarter of the budget, are not effectively alleviating economic, health and social problems. Considers most public officials more concerned with their own problems than with social dilemmas. Calls for income maintenance policies primarily directed to the poor.

014   Binstock, R.H. (1972). Interest-group liberalism and the politics of aging. The Gerontologist, 12(3), 265-280.
Argues forcefully that advocacy organizations in aging fail to address the problems of the severely disadvantaged aging and suggests the need for "a new, forceful coalition." Note: A related editorial by Jerome Kaplan appears on p.212 of the same journal.

015   Browne, W.P.; Olson, L.K. (Eds.). (1983). Aging and public policy: The politics of growing old in America. Westport CT: Greenwood Press, 266p.
Complains that gerontologists have sorely neglected political dimensions of aging issues, and offers chapters on topics including women's issues, national interest groups, Congressional practices, rural inequities, women's concerns, and economics of aging. Extensive bibliography and chapter notes.

016   Butler, R.N. (1978). The economics of aging: We are asking the wrong questions. In: Hubbard, J.P. (Ed.). The economics of aging: The economic, political and social implications of growing old in America: Issues book, Washington DC: The National Journal, 65-70.
Questions "reductionist" attitudes and proposals arising from high Federal costs for aging programs. Points to pressures for early retirement, high health costs to the elderly even with Medicare, and intergenerational benefits from public programs. Argues that adequate Federal funding of research may reduce or contain sums spent on aging.

017   Butler, R.N. (1975). Why survive? Being old in America. New York: Harper & Row, 496p.
Public policy considerations mesh with author's description of social, economic, and psychological difficulties facing elderly. Many statistics and program descriptions are somewhat dated, but general truths they illustrate largely persist. Attacking pacification as a policy goal, author calls for widespread political activism by elderly. His 15 policy goals emphasize priority reordering and elimination of poverty and malnutrition. Thoroughly documented. Bibliography.

018   Butler, R.N. (1969). Age-ism: Another form of bigotry. The Gerontologist, 9(4), 243-246.
Resident resistance to a Federally-assisted housing project for the elderly gives rise to the author's use of the term "age-ism," described as "a deep-seated

uneasiness on the part of the young and the middle-aged" to their own aging process and their fear of age-related powerlessness. Medicare, Social Security, and public housing criticized as "examples of tokenism."

019   Cain, L.D. (1974). The growing importance of legal age in determining the status of the elderly. The Gerontologist, 14(2), 167-174.
An excellent review of the proliferation of legislation and other public actions establishing age criteria related to Federal programs, resulting in a "jungle of age status asychronization." Valuable historical background. Includes a contradiction of the frequently cited statement that Bismarck set 65 as the age for annuity eligibility in Germany. Actually, it may have been 71.

020   Cain, L.D. (1974). Political factors in the emerging legal status of the elderly. In: Eisele, F.R. (Ed.). The political consequences of aging. The Annals of the American Academy of Political and Social Science, 415 (September), 70-79.
Asserts that a separate legal status for the elderly is taking form because much national policy accepts the elderly as unequal and enacts laws designed to overcome the negative consequences of that inequality. Predicts court tests of chronological age to establish special treatment of elderly.

021   Califano, J.A. (1978). The aging of America: Questions for the four-generation society. The Annals of the American Academy of Political and Social Science. 438, 96-107.
An historically significant call by a US Secretary of Health, Education, and Welfare for policy adjustments and fresh thinking to deal with issues arising from the "graying" of the Federal budget. Asks whether trend toward earlier retirement can be maintained, whether income security programs should restructure, whether Medicare and Medicaid can keep up with inflationary health care costs, and how Federal policy can give greater support to family caregiving.

022   Chusid, J.; Horowitz, M. (1984). Broken promises: A report on the state of the elderly during the Reagan Administration. Washington DC: National Council of Senior Citizens; American Federation of State, County, and Municipal Employees, 238p.
A critical examination of Federal budget reductions in Medicare, Social Security and other programs serving older Americans. Especially useful for its state-by-state analyses of cutback impacts.

023   Clark, R.L.; Menefee, J.A. (1981). Federal expenditures for the elderly: Past and future. The Gerontologist, 21(2), 132-137.
Population aging is cited as a major reason for growth of Federal aging programs, but note is taken also of specific Congressional collective decisions on age-related spending from 1960-78. Inflation factors measured. Projections of future outlays presented.

024   Clemente, F. (1975). Age and the perception of national priorities. The Gerontologist, 15(1), 61-63.
A national sample (N=1,504) reports a young (18-39) and middle-aged (40-59) cohorts were more positive on national funding in five areas--health, the environment, drugs, defense, and education--than elderly (60+) respondents. Author "taken aback" by low support by the aged for health.

025   Cohen, E.S. (1976). The US Senate Special Committee on Aging: Victim of age-ism? (Editorial). The Gerontologist, 16(6), 489-90.
Challenges a Senate proposal, later defeated, to merge the Committee on Aging into larger standing committees. Background of the Committee and its importance in inspiring development of a similar House Committee described in a letter from Senate Committee Chairman Frank Church.

026   Cohen, E.S. (1974). Legal research issues on aging. The Gerontologist, 14(3), 263-267.
A useful summary of the rise in organized attention to questions of rights and law, most related directly to Federal programs intended to serve older Americans. Suggests an analytical framework for future research efforts; lists research goals on legal issues rather than substantive legislative matters.

027   Cohen, E.S. (1970). Toward a social policy on aging. The Gerontologist, 10(4), Pt. II, 13-21.
Social policy, described as "the synthesis of competing objectives contending within the framework of a social philosophy conditioned by a value system or system," is viewed as erratic and often contradictory in aging. A call is made for systematic approaches to identify knowledge gaps and to link research to social policy and action.

028   Cohen, E.S. (1962). The state unit on aging: A point of view on structure. The Gerontologist, 2(1), 14-17.
A useful summary of state initiatives made before the Older Americans Act of 1965 required establishment of state units. States typically had established independent governor's committees or commissions; author argues for placing units within the regular framework of state government.

029   Cook, F.L; Kramek, L.M. (1986). Measuring economic hardship among older Americans. The Gerontologist, 26(1), 38-47.
Questions use of poverty level to measure hardship. Reports on telephone survey of 1,422 Chicago residents in 1983 to examine food, housing, or access to medical care difficulties. Elderly respondents no more likely to suffer hardship than adults of other ages, for reasons requiring further analysis. Authors argue for governmental service targeting to subgroups still demonstrably in need of material help.

030   Cook, F.L. (1979). Who should be helped? Public support for social services. Beverly Hills CA: Sage Publications, 227p.
A cross-section of Chicagoans is surveyed in 1976-77 to examine opinions regarding welfare state choices in a context of increasing scarcity and conflict. The rigorous survey methodology reveals that the elderly are preferred over children, and children over adults under 65. Author concludes public is not, willy-nilly, against public spending in the welfare domain, even during tax-cutting era.

031   Cottrell, W.E. (1962). Organization of Federal programs for the aging. The Gerontologist, 2(4), 176-178.
Questions proposals to establish a free-standing Federal Commission on Aging to become advocate and program coordinator. Gives useful detail on work of the Special Staff on Aging then playing an active role within the Department of Health, Education, and Welfare.

032   Cottrell, F. (1960). Government functions and the politics of age. In: Tibbitts, C. (Ed.). Handbook of social gerontology. University of Chicago Press. 624-65.
Discusses "how government has changed and is likely to change in the future in terms of the things it is doing for older people." Valuable for details on burgeoning Federal and state response in the 1950s, including actions and staff alignments within the Department of Health, Education, and Welfare.

033   Coulter, O. (Ed.) (1972). Trends in aging: 1961-1971. Aging, No.212, 8-12.
A summary of papers prepared by the 1971 White House Conference on Aging staff on policy trends since the 1961 conference. Topics include: education, employment and retirement, health care, housing, income, nutrition, retirement roles, spiritual well-being, transportation, facilities and services, government and non-government organizations, planning, research and demonstration, and training.

034   Cowgill, D.O. (1979). The revolution of age. In: Monk, A. (Ed.). The age of aging: A reader in social gerontology. Buffalo NY: Prometheus Press, 63-72.
Challenges argument that greater public policy commitment to aging will cause a severe burden on younger generations. Cites his study of 82 countries in varying states of development and concludes that a rise in the proportion of elderly is inevitably accompanied by decline in ratio of the young. Criticizes pressures for early retirement.

035   Cowgill, D.O. (1972). Aging in American society. In: Cowgill, D.O.; Holmes, L.D. Aging and Modernization. New York: Appleton-Century-Crofts. 243-262.
American society, highly modernized and individualistic, tends to deprive the older person of an important role, that of instructor and arbiter of tradition. This, and a fundamental ambivalance about aging even among the aged, is reflected in inconsistent policies and relatively few privileges attached to age per se. Retirement is often a limbo rather than a desired outcome.

036   Crystal, S. (1982). America's old age crisis: Public policy and the two worlds of aging. New York: Basic Books, 232p.
Public policy depicted as a major contributing factor to growing gap between the best-off and worst-off elderly, at a time when their benefits command an increasingly large budget share. Recommends far-reaching changes in the retirement income and health care systems and greater flexibility in long term care needs. Numerous references and good bibliography.

037   Curtin, S.R. (1972). Nobody ever died of old age: In praise of old people; in outrage at their loneliness. Boston: Little, Brown, and Co., 228p.
An angry account of societal downgrading of older people, as compounded by an often authoritarian, unresponsive social welfare system. Author cites individual experiences of persons ill-served by social, housing and mental health services. Nursing homes, even good ones, regarded as dehumanizing. Chapter 12 advises vigorous consciousness-raising, led by the elderly.

038   Cutler, N.B. (1981). The aging population and social policy. In: Davis, R.H. (Ed.). Aging: Prospects and issues, Third edition. Los Angeles: University of Southern California Press, 236-59.

Dynamics of demographic change influencing sociopolitical trends, but the inter-connectedness is often ignored or misunderstood. Raising or lowering of retirement age seen as an example of far-reaching change, but its consequences are not fully understood. Dependency ratios discussed.

039   Davis, R.H. (Ed.). (1981). Aging: Prospects and issues. Third edition. Los Angeles: University of Southern California Press, 427p.
Intended to reach a broad audience, well-chosen papers deal with social policy issues including Congressional responsiveness and advocacy in chapters 14-18, and "Aging and Society" issues including community services and ethnic considerations in chapters 5-8.

040   Eisdorfer, C. (1978). Societal response to aging: Some possible consequences. In: Jarvik, L. (Ed.) Aging into the 21st Century: Middle-agers today. New York: Gardner Press, Inc. 123-136.
An "insidiously emerging issue" asks whether any society will continue to bear economic and social consequences of older populations regarded as nonproductive. Potentially positive steps would help the elderly contribute as outspoken and vigorous leaders for change and as workers with access to modified working ar-rangements, aided by new forms of education.

041   Eisele, F.R. (Ed.). (1974). The political consequences of aging. The Annals of the American Academy of Political and Social Science. 415(September), 211p.
A worthwhile collection of policy analyses representing a cross-section of ideolo-gies and viewpoints. The editor describes their perspectives as "long range, attempting to situate and analyze the issues in their broader historical context." Topics range from individual programs to demographic and social trends.

042   Estes, C.L.; Newcomer, R.J. (and associates). (1983). Fiscal austerity and aging-shifting government responsibility for the elderly. Beverly Hills, CA: Sage Publications. 278pp.
Offers empirical evidence, much of it conducted by the Aging Health Policy Center at the University of California in San Francisco from 1981-1983, examining consequences of evolving Federal, state and local policies. Concludes that auster-ity, and shift of significant Federal responsibilities to states are causing severe problems.

043   Estes, C.L. (1979). The aging enterprise. San Francisco. Jossey-Bass, 281p.
Challenges aging policy based on assumption that the aged constitute a separate, distinct class, poorly served by a services strategy rather than more far-reaching actions putting priority on greatest need. Older Americans Act, closely inspected, held up as example of "goal displacement," or failure to meet stated objectives. Notable for strong theoretical underpinnings and spirited advoca-cy; excellent references.

044   Etheredge, L. (1984). Aging society and the Federal deficit. Milbank Memorial Fund Quarterly: 62(4), 521-543.
Federal policy on aging, "highly successful and expensive," needs reconsideration in view of the Federal deficit and improved living standards for many elderly. Far-reaching changes will depend on whether national policy succeeds in slowing rise of health costs and improving retirement security.

045   Fischer, D.H. (1977). Growing old in America. New York: Oxford University Press, 242p.
An informative account of changing attitudes and policies toward aging, dating from 1607. Chapter 4—Old Age becomes a Social problem, 1907-1970—is a fairly detailed account of growing Federal concern and action. Chapter 5— A Thought for the Future--rejects Social Security as "unfair to the elderly and expensive to the young." A proposal is advanced for a "national inheritance plan" that would grant a sum in youth; difficulties recognized.

046   Fries, J.F. (1984). The compression of morbidity: Miscellaneous comments about a theme. The Gerontologist, 24(4), 354-359.
An examination, and rejection, of criticisms of author's argument three years earlier that the onset of significant morbidity may be postponed to more closely coincide with termination of the genetic lifespan. Acknowledging a need to increase resources for an increasingly elderly population, this commentary nevertheless reiterates arguments on efficacy of health promotion activities.

047   Fries, J.F. (1981). Aging, natural death, and the compression of morbidity. In: Somers, A.R.; Fabian, D.R. (Eds.). The geriatric imperative: An introduction to gerontology and clinical geriatrics. New York, Appleton-Century-Crofts, 105-116. (Reprinted from the New England Journal of Medicine, 303:1980. 130-135.)
Predicts that the average period of diminished physical vigor will decrease as population aging continues. Concludes that high level medical technology applied at the end of a natural lifespan "epitomizes the absurd", and that human interaction, rather than heroic care, is needed at time of the "terminal drop."

048   Geiger, H.J. (1980). Elder health and social policies: Prelude to a decade of disaster. Generations, 4(2), 11-12, 52.
Pressures for Federal program cost containment are accused of creating "the probability that—in exact parallel to general social policy--medical cost containment, like general budget balancing, will take place on the back of the poor and the elderly." High-technology and other expensive health/social services will be protected but ambulatory and preventive services are likely to suffer.

049   Gelfand, D.E.; Olsen, J.K. (1980). The aging network: Programs and services. New York: Springer Publishing Co., 340p.
Gives basic information about a wide range of programs, emphasizing regional service delivery variations. Older Americans Act closely analyzed; a chapter by Jules Berman summarizes income maintenance programs.

050   Gold, B.; Kutza, E.; Marmor, T. (1977). US social policy on old age. In: Neugarten, B.L.; Havighurst, R.J. (Eds.) (1977). Social policy, social ethics, and the aging society. Committee on Human Development, University of Chicago. GPO 038-000-00299-6, 9-21. (For the National Science Foundation.)
Argues that future policymakers must question the wisdom of programming around a constituency group rather than a problem area.

051   Gordon, T.J. (1979). Prospects for aging in America. In: Riley, M.W. (Ed.). Aging from birth to death: Interdisciplinary perspectives. Washington DC: American Association for the Advancement of Science, 179-197.
A report on a Futures Group study of social and policy consequences of changes in lifespan expectancies, biomedical technologies, and other trends likely by the year 2000. New communications technology seen as having profound effects.

052   Hackett, D.H. (1978) Putting our heads to the "problem" of old age. In: Gross, R.; Gross, B.; Seidman, S. (Eds.). The new old: Struggling for decent aging. Garden City NY: Anchor Books, 58-62.
American history has seen young as the victims of the old and old as the victims of young. Public policy and social change should not seek a new reversal but should look to "a future without victims altogether," one in which an end is put to age discrimination. Social Security is regarded as "fundamentally unsound," imposing "an increasingly heavy and regressive burden on the young."

053   Hapgood, D. (1976). The aging are doing better. In: Gross, R.; Gross, B.; Seidman, S. The new old: Struggling for decent aging. Garden City NY: Anchor Books, 345-363.
Attributes legislative successes to organized advocacy and public support of aging programs. Warns that the twin blocks of enforced retirement and age discrimination are still in need of policy attention. Gives examples of positive programs for older workers, housing, and nursing home reform.

054   Harootyan, R.A. (1981). Interest groups and the development of Federal legislation affecting older persons. In: Hudson, R.B. (Ed.). The aging in politics: Process and policy. Springfield IL: Charles C. Thomas, 74-85.
Legitimate needs have made a case for the elderly's being "included among the faultlessly poor." But many persons who do not meet chronological age requirements are unserved. It is necessary to "move away from dictatorship of the birth certificate" and to enlist the help of the deprived in meeting their own needs on their own terms.

055   Harris, L., and associates. (1981). Aging in the eighties: America in transition, a national poll. Washington DC: National Council on the Aging, 170p.
Finds that most Americans (54 percent) look toward government and the children of the elderly (46 percent) to assume greater responsibility for older people. A slim majority, 51 percent, thought government programs should be available only to low-income elders, but 64 percent thought Social Security should be an exception to this standard. (Questions similar to those asked in 1974 NCOA-Harris poll, The Myth and Reality of Aging in America, permit comparisons on many issues.)

056   Havighurst, R.J. (Chairman). (1969). Research and development goals in social gerontology: A report of a special committee of the Gerontological Society. The Gerontologist, 9(4), Pt.II, 90p.
With funding from the Administration on Aging, the Gerontological Society surveyed existing research related to social policy and societal practices. This report, focusing on applied social gerontology, summarizes initial findings on: work, leisure and education—flexible life styles; living arrangements—ecology; social services; and the economics of aging. A supplementary report (pp.81-90) describes components of a policy-oriented research approach.

057   Hickey, T.; Davies, C.T. (1972). The White House Conference on Aging: An exercise in policy formulation. Aging and Human Development, 3(1), 233-238.
A one-year study of participants in preliminary community conferences in 11 rural Pennsylvania counties and 100 state delegates to the 1971 national conference reveals sharp differences in views of local level participants and final recommendations. Grassroots policy evolution "in this case was a charade."

058   Hubbard, J.P. (Ed.). (1980). Aging: Agenda for the eighties. Conference pro-
        ceedings. Washington DC: The National Journal. 95p.
Sharp disagreement often flares in major addresses and lively discussion, on such
recurrent themes as the future of Social Security, conflicting goals in health care,
consumerism in later years, international comparisons, and age irrelevance. A Senator describes his topic as "the politics of conflict and confusion."

059   Hubbard, J.P. (Ed.). (1979). The economics of aging: The economic, political
        and social implications of growing old in America: Conference proceedings.
        Washington DC: The National Journal, 87p.
Conflicting views on extent and nature of Federal responsibilities to its aging population, with special emphasis on Social Security, are prominent in this informative,
largely verbatim account of a significant conference. Wide range of programs,
topics come under discussion.

060   Hubbard, J.P. (Ed.). (1979). Aging: Agenda for the eighties. Issues book. Wash-
        ington DC. The National Journal, 53p.
Eight articles offering a variety of subjects and outlooks on topics including analysis of Federal aging policy, women's changing roles, lopsided outlays for
institutional care as compared to in-home or ambulatory care/support; employment,
demographics, consumer issues, and age or need entitlement in Federal programs.

061   Hubbard, J.P. (Ed.). (1978). The economics of aging: The economic, political
        and social implications of growing old in America: Issues book, Washington
        DC: The National Journal, 70p.
A collection of Journal articles and papers presenting differing views on policy
issues, most of them related to a fundamental theme: What can the Government
afford to allocate to aging without eroding its ability to serve other sectors of
the population?

062   Hudson, R.B.; Strate, J. (1985). Aging and political systems. In: Binstock,
        R.H.; Shanas, E. (Eds.). Handbook of aging and the social sciences. New York:
        Van Nostrand Reinhold Company, 554-585.
Identifies six factors affecting aging policy: economic and ecological developments,
political culture and structure, public input including citizen and organizational
demands, political elites affecting the timing and direction of policy initiatives,
the framework provided by existing policies and programs, and the workings of the
capitalist market economies and allied social control mechanisms.

063   Hudson, R.B. (Ed.). (1984). The new politics of aging. Generations, 9(1),
        Entire Issue, 56p.
Articles by guest authors in this quarterly journal of the Western Gerontological
Society (now the American Society on Aging) pinpoint policies subject to intensive
pressures in what editor Hudson calls a "shove-push situation where different perceptions of human need, resources availability, and governmental role form a
kaleidoscope of options" among crisis-oriented policymakers. Senior lobby in Washington state discussed.

064   Hudson, R.B. (Ed.). (1981). The aging in politics: Process and policy. Spring-
        field IL: Charles C. Thomas, 294p.
Aging as a lively and increasingly important factor in the political process is the
theme of analyses by authors with varying viewpoints. Impact of contemporary
social, demographic, and economic trends is generally recognized as causing
complex new challenges to aging advocates, who are advised to "work harder than
ever before" to make the case for new forms of action.

065   Hudson, R.B. (1978). The "graying" of the Federal budget and its conse-
       quences for old-age policy. The Gerontologist, 18(5), 428-440.
A landmark critique arguing that rising costs of public policies targeted for older
persons, improved well-being of the aggregate older population, and higher total
benefits to older persons as compared to other age groups undermine "the political
legitimacy and utility of the aging." A new policy system is sought to prevent the
old-old, the minority old, and widows from becoming victims of retrenchment
pressures.

066   Hudson, R.B. (1978). Political and budgetary consequences of an aging popu-
       lation. In: Hubbard, J.P. (Ed.). The economics of aging: The economic, polit-
       ical and social implications of growing old in America: Issues book,
       Washington DC: The National Journal, 44-50.
A useful updating of a theme expressed earlier by the same author (see 065)
adding later developments and again warning that growing resistance to across-
the-board Federal attention to the elderly could cause neglect of the most vulnerable of the older population.

067   Johnson, H.R.; Maddox, G.L.; Kaplan, J. (1982). Three perspectives on the
       1981 White House Conference on Aging. The Gerontologist, 22(2), 125-128.
Prominent Gerontological Society members who took part in conference activities
give their views. Johnson reports clear support for education in gerontology,
despite "the chaos and controversy." Maddox finds that the Conference Committee
on Research "highlighted a broad range of concerns" and priorities. Kaplan detects
delegates' concern about uncertain Federal support of services.

068   Johnson, L.B. (1967). Aid for the aged: Message from the President of the
       United States. US House of Representatives, 90th Congress, 1st Session, Docu-
       ment No.40, Jan. 23, 9p.
Asks raising of Social Security benefits "to a level which will better meet today's
needs," improvement and extending of health care available to the elderly, an
"attack on the roots of unjust discrimination," and renewal and expansion of programs "to help bring fulfillment and meaning in retirement years." Social Security
benefits called "grossly inadequate." Calls for expanded home health services.

069   Kalish, R.A. (1979). The new ageism and the failure models: A polemic. The
       Gerontologist, 19(4), 398-402.
Stereotypes of "the elderly" may be used even by their advocates to picture them
as "the least capable, least healthy, and least alert," standing in need of support
from professionals. Another consequence, it is argued, is development of services
that may limit self-determination. Policymakers are listed among those who may
perpetuate the failure model; author prefers a personal growth model of aging.

070   Kaplan, J. (1973). Revenue sharing: Myth or reality for the aged? (Editorial)
       The Gerontologist, 13(3). p.274.
Criticizes The State and Local Fiscal Assistance Act of 1972, then in its second
year, for an apparent "spottiness and dearth in aged services response." Moreover,
"Experience to date again suggests unless funds are mandated for aging use, the
aged do not fare well in the general funding marketplace."

071   Kennedy, J.F. (1963). Elderly citizens of our nation: Message from the President of the United States. US House of Representatives, 88th Congress, 1st session. Document No.72, Feb. 21, 16p.
Declares all levels of government must "act vigorously to improve the lot of our aged." Hospital insurance through Social Security seen as "reasonable and practical." Improvements asked in Social Security, employment opportunities housing, community action, and a pilot food stamp program. Goal is not to segregate elderly but to present facts about older citizens, including their "unutilized potential."

072   Kent, D.P. (1967). John F. Kennedy's reflections on aging. The Gerontologist, 7(3), p.146, 223.
A compilation from Kennedy statements before and during his presidency, ranging from use of leisure time to a call for care of the chronically ill in their own homes. A 1963 paper declared: "Rules of employment that are based on the calendar rather than ability are not good rules, nor are they realistic."

073   Kent, D.P. (1965). Aging—Fact and fancy. The Gerontologist, 5(2), 51-56, 111.
A classic warning by a pioneer in aging (then Director of the US Office on Aging) about the "chasm between our perceptions of aging and the facts," and the frequent mismatch between false assumptions and public program objectives.

074   Kent, D.P. (1962). Progress for older people—how far in the coming decade? The Gerontologist, 2(4), 196-200.
An appraisal by the Federal Special Assistant for Aging at an especially challenging time to aging policy. All Federal programs on aging said to account for only three percent of gross national product; "tragically low income of older people" challenged. A "mighty mobilization" of thought and effort called for.

075   Kent, D.P. (1961). The White House Conference in retrospect. The Gerontologist, 1(1), 4-7.
A straightforward account by a leader in social gerontology, emphasizing "a vast national effort" preceding the conference at state and other levels. Cites a conference theme, "Older people are not a race apart from the rest of mankind," adding: "While programs specifically tailored to meet special needs are necessary, these should be an integrated aspect of society."

076   Kerschner, P.A. (1977). Changing legislation: Its effect on programs. In: Davis, R.H. (Ed.). Aging: Prospects and Issues. (Revised, Fourth Printing.) Los Angeles: Andrus Gerontolgy Center, 152-163.
Pays close attention to Federal policy development between 1963-73, with special reference to the origins of the Older Americans Act, Congressional misgivings about the status of the Administration on Aging, and the early challenges facing the aging network established in the 1973 Older Americans Act amendments. Succinct housing, health summaries also informative.

077   Kerschner, P.A.; Hirschfield, I.S. (1975). Public policy and aging: Analytic approaches. In: Woodruff, D.S.; Birren, J.E. (Eds.). Aging: Scientific Perspectives and Social Issues. New York: D. Van Nostrand Co., 352-373.
Identifies four dichotomies on which legislation is often based: categorical vs. generic; holistic vs. segmented; crisis vs. rational, and political contest vs. future planning. Relationships to existing programs discussed; improvements proposed.

078   Klemmack, D.L.; Roff, L.L. (1981). Predicting general and comparative sup-
       port for government's providing benefits to older persons. The Gerontologist,
       21(6), 592-599.
An Alabama probability sample (N=1,015) in 1979 expresses substantial support for
more services and benefits, prominently expressed in the Federal budget. The correlation when such expenditures are compared to other possible public funding,
however, is low. Authors find that "the priority placed on benefits for older persons is tenuous and may be subject to radical shifts."

079   Klemmack, D.L.; Roff, L.L. (1980). Public support for age as an eligibility
       criterion for programs for older persons. The Gerontologist, 20(2), 148-153.
Ten Federal and state age-only eligibility programs receive support from an Alabama sample (N=332), when it is believed that there are few alternatives other
than government for necessary services. Advocates may face contradiction: building
a positive image, while arguing that needy elderly are deserving of help.

080   Kutza, E.A. (1981). The benefits of old age: Social welfare policy for the
       elderly. Chicago: The University of Chicago Press, 187p.
Synthesizes policy considerations in eight programs: Old Age and Survivors Insurance, taxation treatment, Medicare, Older Americans Act, Supplemental Security
Income, Medicaid, food stamps, and housing subsidies. Effects of multiple benefits
examined. Age-based programming questioned; ways of integrating public programs
and private aid discussed.

081   Lammers, W.W.; Klingman, D. (1984). State policies and the aging: Sources,
       trends, and options. Lexington MA: Lexington Books, 252p.
Federal-state partnership programs dominate this analysis of state efforts from
1955-75. Means of measuring "aging policy effort" explained. States chosen for
close examination: California, Washington, Minnesota, Iowa, Ohio, Maine, North
Carolina, and Florida. States seen as likely base for aging advocacy, having more
policy leeway in future, targeting assistance to most needy.

082   Lammers, W.W. (1983). Public policy and the aging. Washington DC: CQ
       Press, 265p.
To emphasize diversity among older Americans, portraits of five citizens presented,
pinpointing program inadequacies in meeting needs. Policy development, and the
roles of executives, bureaucracies, and legislatures described. United States called
laggard in income maintenance and health insurance. Potential for improved status
of older workers seen; housing and social services called politically vulnerable.
1980s policy agenda presented. 12 pages of references.

083   Lammers, W.W. (1981). Congress and the aging. In: Davis, R.H. (Ed.).   Aging:
       Prospects and issues, Third edition. Los Angeles: University of Southern Cali-
       fornia Press, 274-296.
Gives decade-by-decade account of legislation on aging from the "slow start" in
the early 60s through the early 1980s. A useful, if brief, treatment of changing
Congressional priorities. Attention given to the influence of state experiments on
Federal policy.

084   Lammers, W.W. (1978). Aged-based program eligibility in the legislative pro-
       cess: Conflict patterns and implications for change. Los Angeles: Andrus
       Gerontology Center. 71p.
Recognizes frequent arbitrariness of age-based criteria, but argues for caution in

revisions of such standards. Estimates the amount and nature of legislative conflict likely to arise if age as a criterion in policies affecting the elderly are modified or replaced.

085   Leadership Council of Aging Organizations. (1982). An analysis of the 1981 White House Conference on Aging. Washington DC: 55p.
Cross-referenced summaries of key proposals from 700 recommendations adopted by 14 conference committees provide helpful linkages. Special attention is paid to income security, described as causing "most of the controversy at the conference." Other major categories: health, social services/housing, and special concerns (older women, rural needs, minority elderly, research and education).

086   Levine, M. (1980). Research in law and aging. The Gerontologist, 20(2), 163-167.
A helpful review of legal research issues that often arise in the workings of Federal aging programs. Predicts that major changes can be expected in legal rules, government programs, and legally-facilitated social customs. At the heart of the field of law and aging is the question of whether the law should take chronological old age into account, or whether "its use is an invidious discrimination, like differential treatment on the basis of race, religion or national origin."

087   Lowy, L. (1980) Social policies and programs on aging: What is and what should be in the later years. Lexington MA: Lexington Books. 269p.
A well-rounded analysis of public social policy, posing significant questions on the eve of the 1981 White House Conference on Aging. Influence of policy on practitioners emphasized; 18-point program presented. Older Americans Act seen as most significant Federal action on aging since 1935 enactment of Social Security. Need seen for social services as "an equal partner to... health." Other topics: housing, income, self-determination by elders. Extensive bibliography.

088   Manton, K.G. (1986). Past and future life expectancy increases at later ages: Their implications for the linkage of chronic morbidity, disability, and mortality. Journal of Gerontology, 42(5), 672-681.
Finds considerable future potential for increasing life expectancy by controlling major known risk factors, but that causes of disability differ from causes of mortality. Suggests reconsideration of earlier projections of disability levels for the old-old, and current relations of mortality and disability may not hold at more advanced ages, with significant consequences for social and health policy.

089   Markson, E.W.; Batra, G.R. (Eds.) (1980) Public policies for an aging population. Lexington MA: Lexington Books, 141p.
Themes selected to reflect broad concerns about aging policy, rather than "global approaches" or "over-specificity dictated by a particular discipline." Economic development and self-directed approaches to community service use among topics considered.

090   Meyner, R.B. (1961.) The responsibilities of government. In: US Department of Health, Education, and Welfare. Aging with a future. 17-25.
The Governor of New Jersey, in a paper prepared for the White House Conference on Aging, declares "the Federal system is weakened when the national Government does not accept and fulfill its share of the obligations." Calls for the Social Security system to provide medical insurance for the elderly. Sees need for Federal, state coordinating mechanisms in comprehensive aging programs.

**091 Miller, B.K. (1980). Pluralist politics have limitations. Generations (Special
        issue on public policy), 4(1), 31-32.**
Declares that pluralism, or pursuit of relatively narrow interest group objectives,
has emphasized "supposedly unique needs of the aged" while claiming that such
needs require substantially more attention than do those of other deprived groups.

**092 Miller. M. (Ed.). (1981). Policy issues for the elderly poor. US Community
        Services Administration, CSA Pamphlet 6172-8, 121p.**
The successor agency to the US Office of Economic Opportunity summarizes facts
needed "to provide a framework for policy development" helpful to low-income
older persons. Contributing authors deal with income adequacy, energy costs,
minority group issues, the rural elderly, and the need for a comprehensive assessment of the elderly poor.

**093 Minkler, M.; Estes, C.L. (Eds.). (1984). Readings in the political economy of
        aging. Farmingdale NY: Baywood Publishing Company, 278p.**
Our society's "aging problem" is depicted as a structural one, engendered by
society's differential treatment of the aged as a group. The "political economy"
view of aging concludes that separatist thinking about the elderly results in policy
failure to address root causes of aging-related problems. Guest authors deal with
health, women's issues, old age economic security, retirement practices, and future
social policy. Well-chosen, numerous references.

**094 Monk, A. (1982). Age integrated or age segregated approaches to service
        development for the aged. Paper presented at session in "Interfamily Rela-
        tions," Tenth International Conference of Social Gerontology, Deauville,
        France, 19p.**
Questions age integration as a guiding principle for aging policymaking arguing 1)
the aged often encounter disadvantages when served in agencies that ignore categorical distinctions, 2) service providers are often imbued with a nihilistic attitude
toward old age and prefer to serve younger persons, and 3) the very organization
of generic services often discourages their use by the elderly.

**095 Morris, R. (1980). Social welfare policy and aging: Implications for the
        future—Between the good earth and pie in the sky. In: Markson, E.W.; Batra,
        G.R. Public policies for an aging population. Lexington MA: Lexington Books,
        121-131.**
Social policy called "a general sense of direction," not particular programs. A
major goal is to enhance control over one's life. Government regarded not solely
as a "financing faucet" but as socially responsible for the quality and effects of
its work. Area agencies on aging urged to act as "meaningful planning control
mechanisms in the evolution of other social programs."

**096 Morris, R. (1966). Viewpoint: Gerontological research and social policy. The
        Gerontologist, 6(1), 2-3.**
Asserts that research has not yet provided answers for "plaguesome questions" on
key issues related to needs and roles. Hope expressed that newly enacted Older
Americans Act will provide a new instrument for adaptation of research findings
to policy formulation.

**097 National Association of State Units on Aging. (1981). Major themes of the
        state White House conferences on aging. Washington DC: 14p.**
Identifies 51 recommendations made at state conferences held as preludes to the
1981 White House Conference. More than 37,000 persons, most of them 55+, dealt

with varied issues at the state events but reached consensus on a significant number. Many recommendations, however, were state specific.

098   Nathanson, P. (1984). Future trends in aging and the law. Generations, 8(3), 7-9.
Role of lawsuits and advocacy efforts in helping to "humanize the bureaucratic maze often forced upon the elderly" described. Asserts that litigative process may no longer be the arena for major reform; advocacy directed at state legislatures may play larger role.

099   National Council on the Aging. (1982). Leadership Council gets most of its "8 for the 80s" list. Perspective on Aging, 11(1), 10-12, 30.
Reports that the Leadership Council of Aging Organizations was successful in winning support at the 1981 White House Conference on Aging for an 8-point policy program advanced by Council. Specific council recommendations are compared with proposals from individual conference committees.

100   Nelson G.M. (1982.) Social class and public policy for the elderly. Social Service Review. March 1982. 85-107.
Sees uneven Federal response to three groups of the elderly: the poor or marginal, middle- and lower-middle "downwardly mobile," and the middle- and upper-middle income. Proposed redistribution of benefits would remove health barriers, alleviate poverty, reform services.

101   Nelson, G.M. (1982). Support for the aged: Public and private responsibility. Social Work, 27(2), 137-143.
An incisive analysis, primarily focused on caregiving, but applies underlying principles to numerous public service programs. Adequate income for the aged viewed as key element of good family policy. Federal adjustments suggested "to elicit and facilitate the cooperation of family and community helping networks...".

102   Neugarten, B.L., (Ed.) (1983.) Age or need? Public policies for older people. Beverly Hills: Sage Publications, 288p.
Age-targeted Federal programs regarded as central to public debate on how to enhance the welfare of the older population in ways constructive to the whole society. Editor and most guest authors argue for re-examination of programs designed for older people, emphasizing improved circumstances for many of them.

103   Neugarten, B.L. (1979). Policy for the 1980s: Age or need entitlement? In: Hubbard, J.P. (Ed.). (1979). Aging: Agenda for the eighties. Issues book. Washington DC. The National Journal, 48-52.
Sums up author's theme that age has become an increasingly misleading indicator within the highly diversified older population. Thus, "policies and programs formulated on the basis of age are falling increasingly wide of the mark; income and health care and housing and other goods and services should be provided, not according to age, but to need." Subjects age discrimination laws to close analysis.

104   Neugarten, B.L.; Havighurst, R.J. (Eds.) (1977). Social policy, social ethics, and the aging society. Committee on Human Development, University of Chicago. GPO 038-000-00299-6, 119p. Extending the human lifespan: Social policy and social ethics. GPO 038-000-00337-2, 70p. (Both for the National Science Foundation.)

Companion works based on a conference culminating a three-year study of issues related to decisions about the proportion of society's resources dedicated to its aging population. Stimulating, significant exchanges of views on age as an eligibility criterion, commitments to be made for health care and economic security of the elderly, consequences of lifespan extension, other issues.

105   Neugarten, B.L. (1974). Age groups in American society and the rise of the young-old. In: Eisele, F.R. (Ed.). The political consequences of Aging. The Annals of the American Academy of Political and Social Science. 415(September), 187-98.
The rise of the age group 55 to 75, 15 percent of the population, expected to change old stereotypes about aging and have an impact on social and political processes. The majority of old-old will probably live independently but increasing numbers may require supportive services and special physical adjustments.

106   Neugarten, B.L. (1972). Social implications of a prolonged lifespan. The Gerontologist, 12(4), 323-440.
Asks whether major scientific breakthroughs in extending life expectancy would "so aggravate the problems of health, medical care, income and housing housing that the old would be worse off than now?" Urges early attention to ethical issues "of tremendous importance."

107   Newcomer, R.J.; Harrington, C. et al. (1983). Policy developments in the Medicare, Medicaid, and social services programs. San Francisco: Aging Health Policy Center, University of California, 54p.
Broadbased inquiries about effects of funding cutbacks and other policy changes in the early 1980s lead to warnings that Medicare financial solvency may be compromised if significant modifications are not made, that Medicaid cross-state inequities had been intensified, and that gaps in national long term care policy had worsened noninstitutional care problems.

108   Nixon, R.M. (1972.) Making recommendations for action on behalf of older Americans: Message from the President of the United States. House of Representatives, 92nd Congress, 2nd session, Document No.92-268, March 23, 25pp.
A "comprehensive strategy" calls for: protecting income position of elderly; upgrading nursing home quality of care, helping older persons live dignified lives at home by expanding and reforming service programs, and by reorganizing Federal Government aging activities. Supports indexed Social Security benefits, a fivefold rise in Older American Act funds, and multidisciplinary, "comprehensive, coordinated research program."

109   Olson, L.; Caton, C.; Duffy, R. (1981). The elderly and the economy. Lexington MA: Lexington Books, 199p.
Relates prospects for the 65+ population to Data Resources, Inc.'s baseline simulation of the macroeconomic outlook up to 2005, focusing on possible options primarily in income transfer programs and potential changes in job opportunity. Combinations of options also considered. Technical appendix on DRI study.

110   Olson, L.K. (1982). The political economy of aging: The state, private power, and social welfare. New York: Columbia University Press, 270p.
Questions whether "liberal accommodationist reforms" can deal with structural causes of "the current crisis in old age policies and programs." Conversely, conservative program curtailments turn over "solutions to the same private market

forces that have created, and continue to create the social problems of old age." Especially critical of a "medical industrial complex" regarded as unresponsive to real needs of the elderly.

111   Oriol, W.E. (1981). "Modern" old age and public policy. The Gerontologist, 21(1), 35-45.
Reviews Congressional response to aging issues beginning with groundbreaking 1960 report issued by a Senate unit that put high priority on what was to become Medicare. This issue did not stand alone; the Senate Committee on Aging early saw the need for a broad view of interrelated issues. Questions requiring hard thinking in the 1980s briefly described.

112   Oriol, W.E. (1970). Social policy priorities: Age vs. youth—The Federal Government. The Gerontologist, 10(3), 207-210.
Challenges a statement made by a Secretary of Health, Education, and Welfare suggesting that expenditures for the aged were out of balance in comparison to spending for youth. Problems in establishing "a grand design for Federal allocation" discussed; fragmentation of Congressional authority a major factor.

113   Palmore, E. (1976). The future status of the aged. The Gerontologist, 16(4), 297-302.
Uses Census and National Health interview survey data to examine the status of the aged, relative to that of younger groups. Improved key indicators since 1961 show gains have been made and that programs for the aged have had beneficial effects and should be continued. Findings "contradict the theories that the status of the aged continues to decline in modern societies...".

114   Pifer, A. (1986). The public policy response. In: Pifer, A.; Bronte, L. (Eds.). Our aging society: Paradox and promise. New York: W.W. Norton, 391-413.
Concluding commentary in a book produced for the Aging Society Project of the Carnegie Corporation, outlining issues arising from population aging and urging widespread attention to them. The question is not whether government should have a role, but the nature and extent of that role. Apparent policy shift from youth to elderly seen in need of balanced, intergenerational communication; need to enhance productivity of workers in life's "third-quarter" (ages 50-75) stressed.

115   Powell, L.A.; Williamson, J.B. (1985). The Reagan-era shift toward restrictiveness in old age policy in historical perspective. International Journal of Aging and Human Development, 21(2), 81-86.
Identifies a reform period beginning in the 1930s and diminishing from the late 1970s on. Compares this with a 19th Century liberalization and subsequent diminution of relief given to paupers and others in need; identifies the primary objective in both instances as reduction of public expenditures and taxes.

116   Pratt, H.J. (1976). The gray lobby. University of Chicago: 258p.
Regards the Federal Government's response to needs of the nation's elderly in the 1960s and '70s as "remarkable." To describe development of an "old age policy system," author begins with pension movement from 1922-35. Details upsurge of Government/private advocacy from 1960 on, and gives close attention to its success with 1972 Social Security amendments.

117 President's Task Force on the Aging. (1970.) Toward a brighter future for the elderly. Washington DC: 60pp.
Declares "government should act with and on behalf of the elderly much more vigorously than it currently does," in partnership with private and voluntary sectors. Among its 24 recommendations: establish a Presidential Executive Office on Aging, bring all elderly up to the poverty line, abolish the Social Security retirement test, and improve Medicare coverage.

118 Public Policy Center. (1982). Rediscovering governance: Using policy options to address the needs of older Americans: An overview. Menlo Park CA: SRI International, 62p.
Governance is described as collaborative approaches using existing government powers and private sector and community resources, emphasizing changes in rules, regulations, or administration. Examples given of actions in promotion of self-help, employment, transportation, mental health, and social supports. Appendix gives additional examples.

119 Randall, O.A. (1977). Aging in America today: New aspects in aging. The Gerontologist, 17(1), 6-11.
Asks that public policy reflect the diversity and aspirations of older persons, "the most individualistic people alive today." Argues that public policy is often for "the sole aim of saving public dollars at the expense of the people for whom more dollars should be made available."

120 Rich, B.M.; Baum, M. (1984). The aging: A guide to public policy. Pittsburgh: University of Pittsburgh Press: 275p.
A far-ranging analysis, recognizing many program faults and policy contradictions, yet citing "considerable accomplishments" of efforts thus far. The Older Americans Act "aging network" seen as an organizing focus for incremental policymaking. Failure to raise elderly from poverty seen as most significant gap in fragmented Federal policy.

121 Riley, M.W. (1979). Aging, social change, and social policy. In: Riley, M.W. (Ed.). Aging from birth to death: Interdisciplinary perspectives. Washington DC: American Association for the Advancement of Science. 109-121.
"Plasticity" of the aging process, as expressed within and among varying cohorts seen as a force for far-reaching social change: "We are not mired in any ineluctable process of aging." Policy implications discussed.

122 Riley, M.W.; Riley, J.W.; Johnson, M.E. (1969) Introduction. In: Riley, M.W.; Riley, J.W.; Johnson, M.E. Aging and society: Vol.2, Aging and the professions. New York: Russell Sage Foundation. 1-17.
This section of a landmark series of volumes summarizing research findings is directed at professionals likely to become involved in gerontology, but it also includes succinct discussion of standards for allocating resources to older people by governmental programs and societal action, ethical standards arising from legislation, and the balance between needs and services.

123 Rosenfeld, A. (1985). Consequences. In: Rosenfeld, A. Prolongevity II, 247-267.
Potentially negative policy and social effects of scientific breakthroughs to prolong the human lifespan are acknowledged by a science authority who, nevertheless, advocates national gerontological research programs capable of constructive advances in control of the aging process.

124   Rosenwaike, I.; Logue, B. (1985). The extreme aged in America: A portrait of an expanding population. Westport CT: Greenwood Press, 253p.
Includes discussion of public policy considerations arising as the number and proportion of persons of age 85 and over continue its dramatic growth.

125   Rosow, I. (1970). Old people: Their friends and neighbors. In: Shanas, E. (Ed.). Aging in contemporary society. Beverly Hills: Sage Publications. 57-67.
Age segregation as a possible consequence of public programs or social trends is regarded as beneficial in some cases, providing more peers than likely in other settings. Author cites studies showing that friendships and interactions with neighbors increase dramatically among elders who live among other elders.

126   Rosow, I. (1962). Old age: one moral dilemma of an affluent society. The Gerontologist, 2(4), 182-191.
Argues that old age as a major social problem must be viewed as part of the larger social order, which has stripped older persons of roles and advantages found in less advanced societies. Calls for "complete medical care under the Social Security" and indexed, more adequate Social Security.

127   Ruggles, P.; Moon, M. (1985). The impact of recent legislative changes in benefit programs for the elderly. The Gerontologist, 25(2), 153-160.
Analyzes August 1983 Congressional Budget Office data and concludes that benefit reductions of prior two years were concentrated among those with 1982 incomes between $10,000 and $20,000, above the official poverty line. The "fairness" of the cuts is debatable, depending on weight given to complex factors. Findings described as short-run.

128   Samuelson, R.J. (1978.) The elderly: Who will support them? In: Hubbard, J.P. (Ed.). The economics of aging: The economic, political and social implications of growing old in America: Issues Book, Washington DC: The National Journal, 6-11.
A generally skeptical response to the question: How much responsibility should government assume for the elderly? Reports on view that the total dependency ratio will remain about even as elderly proportionately increase and youth declines, but then cites contradictory evidence.

129   Schneider, E.L.; Brody, J.A. (1983). Aging, natural death, and the compression of morbidity: Another view. The New England Journal of Medicine, 309(14), 854-855.
Takes issue with J.F. Fries' predictions (see Entry 047) that chronic disease will occupy a smaller proportion of the lifespan as the human survival curve continues to "rectangularize." Cites evidence that the average period of diminished vigor will probably increase. Urges health and other policymakers to allocate resources accordingly.

130   Schulder, D.J. (1985). Federal programs for older persons—something to celebrate. Perspective on Aging, 14(1). 8-11.
Prompted by the 50th anniversary of Social Security and the 20th anniversary of Medicare, Medicaid and the Older Americans Act, author finds many imperfections but adds: "The Federal network of guarantees and services to the elderly represent at least the minimum of what a decent and caring society should provide in 1985."

131 Sheppard, H.L. (1982). Aging services a right, most say. Perspective on Aging, 11(1), pp.6, 32.
Cites findings from polls indicating support by interviewees (below and above age 65) for government to assume more responsibility for social programs assisting the elderly. Skepticism expressed about ability of private charities and business to fill gaps caused by government cutbacks.

132 Storey, J.R. (1983). Older Americans in the Reagan era: Impacts of Federal policy changes. Washington, DC: Urban Institute Press, 48p.
Finds that Fiscal Year 1981-1983 budgets resulted in substantial benefit and service cuts for the low-income aged. Cumulative effects of even modest cuts described, e.g.: "An SSI [Supplemental Security Income] recipient who receives Food Stamps and lives in subsidized housing may lose up to 5 percent of total income from reduced stamps and higher rents. Such recipients may also lose access to various health, social, and transportation funds if their communities have been unable to make up lost Federal funds."

133 Streib, G.F. (Ed.). (1981). Programs for older Americans: Evaluation by academic gerontologists. Gainesville FL: University Presses of Florida, 268p.
Draws upon reports from participants in the Research Fellowship Program of the Gerontological Society of America for firsthand examinations of varying Federally-supported programs. Particularly valuable insights are provided in a chapter by Charles E. McConnell on an area agency on aging's involvement in an older workers program.

134 Taber, M.; Flynn, M. (1971). Social policy and social provision for the elderly in the 1970s. The Gerontologist, 11(4), Pt. II, 51-54.
A 1968-1969 limited study of 400 agencies, programs, and institutions in three Illinois counties, using a broad framework crossing lines of medical, income maintenance, social services, education, public housing, employment and job retraining, and recreation systems. Direct money payments predominate but are modest; services are sparsely distributed.

135 Tavani, C. (1979). Meeting the needs of the oldest of the old. Aging, Nos. 291-292, 2-7.
Presents arguments for Federal policies that will give special consideration to the oldest of the old. A modest increase in income to the oldest poor seen as "an efficient way of assuring simple but essential personal care assistance" when this is feasible. Other supportive actions offered.

136 The Urban Institute Human Resources and Income Security Project. (1975). Handbook of Federal programs benefiting older Americans: Appendix I in Federal Council on the Aging. The Interrelationships of Benefit Programs for the Elderly, DHEW Pub. 76-20951, 144p.
Thirty-four programs are identified as the most relevant to the elderly population; program descriptions key in on common program elements and help identify interactions. "Myriad benefits" of 1975 are called "a massive set of complex and confusing program regulations and policy objectives."

137 The Urban Institute Human Resources and Income Security Project. (1975). The combined impact of selected benefit programs on older Americans: A TRIM analysis. Appendix III, Federal Council on the Aging. The Interrelationships of Benefit Programs for the Elderly, DHEW Pub. 76-20953, 79p.

Focuses on relationships of three major benefit programs: Supplemental Security Income, Medicaid, and Food Stamps. Changes in any one of the programs are traced through the primary and secondary impacts of the change on individual program benefits and combined benefits from all three programs.

138   The Urban Institute Human Resources and Income Security Project. (1975). Programs for older Americans in four states: A case study of Federal, state, and local benefit programs. Appendix II in Federal Council on the Aging. The Interrelationships of Benefit Programs for the Elderly, DHEW Pub. 76-20952, 70p.

Wisconsin, Georgia, Massachusetts, and Washington are visited for close examination of programs that are illustrative, rather than statistically representative. Level of program activity varies considerably, as do state offices on aging. Eligibility determination a major problem in each state.

139   Tibbitts, C. (1962). Politics of aging: Pressure for change. In: Donahue W.; Tibbitts, C. (Eds.). Politics of age. Ann Arbor MI: University of Michigan Press, 16-17.

Relates rise of legislative concern about aging to rise of advocacy for and by the elderly, predicting a dynamic, continuing relationship between politics and aging.

140   Torrey, B.B. (1985). Sharing increasing costs on declining income: The visible dilemma of the invisible aged. Milbank Memorial Fund Quarterly. 63(2), 377-394.

Foresees rapidly rising Federal per capita costs for the very old, but Federal data about the elderly is aggregated, the old-old are "statistical ghosts" in important respects. Despite this difficulty, author presents analysis of resources and needs of the oldest elders.

141   Uehara, E.S.; Geron, S.; Beeman, S.K. (1986) The elderly poor in the Reagan era. The Gerontologist, 26(1), 48-55.

A sample of Chicago public aid recipients (N=494) is asked in autumn 1983 to describe losses caused by policy changes in cash benefit, health care, and food programs. The Supplemental Security Income (SSI) "safety net" is often unstrung by cutbacks in other programs. Policymakers urged to reach out and assist this vulnerable population.

142   US Congressional Budget Office. (1985). An analysis of selected deficit reduction options affecting the elderly and disabled. (Staff Working Paper) 115p.

An objective analysis, without recommendations, on 16 specific cost-cutting or revenue-raising options related to: reductions in cost-of-living adjustments for non-means-tested programs; increases in premiums or copayments for Medicare enrollees; and taxation of some forms of retirement income.

143   US Congressional Clearinghouse on the Future. (1984). Tomorrow's elderly: Issues for Congress. (For the US House of Representatives, Select Committee on Aging)

Subjects major public programs to examination in light of demographic and other factors; identifies unresolved questions and offers illustrative policy options to stir discussion. Numerous graphics. An important listing, "Historical Patterns and Legislation Affecting the Elderly" suffers from tiny print, but is worth study for its decade-by-decade grouping of policy actions.

144   US Department of Health and Human Services. (1982) <u>Final report of the 1981</u>
      <u>White House Conference on Aging</u>. (Three volumes) 115p., 140p., 204p.
Volume I devoted primarily to chapters on income, health care, social benefits and
services, and research, each concluding with generalized recommendations appar-
ently reflecting Administration views. Volume II provides conference background
and major conference addresses. Volume III gives findings from a post-conference
survey of conference delegates and observers. Actual recommendations of 14 conference committees begin on p.81.

145   US Department of Health, Education and Welfare. (1972). <u>Toward a national</u>
      <u>policy on aging</u>: Proceedings of the 1971 White House Conference on Aging,
      Nov. 28-Dec. 2. 186p., 253p.
Valuable background information and texts of major conference addresses in Volume
I. White House Conference Act of 1968 in Appendix A. Volume II primarily devoted
to what Conference Chairman Arthur Flemming calls a "remarkable set of recommendations" from 14 sections. Reports from 18 Special Concerns Sessions provide
"indepth discussion on topics of specific aspects of aging or of the circumstances
of particular groups...".

146   US Department of Health, Education, Welfare. (1961). <u>The Nation and its</u>
      <u>older people</u>. Report of the White House Conference on Aging, Jan. 9-12,
      1961. 333p.
Summary of conference recommendations in Part 3 identifies the most discussed
problem as "the need for health and medical services in the later years of life."
Reports by 20 sections appear in Part 3. Text of White House Conference on
Aging Act of 1958 appears in Appendix 1.

147   US Federal Council on the Aging. (1975). <u>The interrelationships of benefit</u>
      <u>programs for the elderly</u>. 52p.
In response to 1973 legislation requesting a study, the Council makes recommendations on programs that reduce their benefits as benefits from other programs
increase, income tests used in several programs, asset tests in other programs,
programs with low rates of participation, and administration and program evaluation. The goal is "to move our society towards a system in which all elderly individuals in similar economic circumstances would be treated the same."

148   US General Accounting Office. (1977). <u>The well-being of older people in</u>
      <u>Cleveland, Ohio</u>. HRD-77-70. 100p.
An ambitious survey based on 1,600 interviews of 65+ persons is the basis of this
analysis of the effectiveness of 23 Federal programs the elderly in Cleveland.
Difficulties and shortcomings identified. <u>Note</u>: For a related GAO home health care
study, see Entry 341.

149   US House of Representatives. Select Committee on Aging. (1984). <u>The polit-</u>
      <u>icization of the 1981 White House Conference on Aging</u>. SuDoc Y4Ag4/2:
      W58/6, 140p.
Gives findings from Committee and General Accounting Office investigations of
"inappropriate efforts to control and influence" the 1981 conference. The report is
intended "to prevent future White House Conferences from being politicized."

150   US House of Representatives. Select Committee on Aging. (1979). <u>Federal</u>
      <u>responsibility to the elderly</u>: Executive programs and legislative jurisdiction.
      SuDoc Y4.Ag4/2:E12/6//979.

Charts give details on 48 major Federal programs benefitting the elderly, described in a foreword by Committee Chairman Claude Pepper as "a bewildering maze of programs and regulations that is a nightmare for the elderly person trying to find his or her way through it." Two additional charts list Congressional Committees with aging concerns, and their jurisdictions.

151   US Senate. Select Committee on Presidential Campaign Activities. (1974). Activities regarding the elderly. In: The Final Report. S.Report 93-981. 419-428.
Summarizes findings by the "Watergate" Committee headed by Senator Sam J. Ervin in regard to the "use of Federal resources...employed to secure the support of older Americans" the 1972 Presidential campaign.

152   US Senate. Special Committee on Aging. (1971). Developments in Aging: 1970. Washington DC: S.Report 92-784.
Committee's annual report is directed almost entirely at issues expected to be raised at the 1971 White House Conference on Aging and analysis of recommendations made at the White House Conference. Committee Chairman Frank Church, in preface, raises key questions, calls aging "too dynamic to serve as a tame subject for an inconsequential conference."

153   US Senate. Special Committee on Aging. (1963). Developments in Aging: 1959 to 1963. S.Report 8. 224p.
Gives reasons for Senate decision to establish special unit to carry on work of prior subcommittee (see entries 154 and 155). Reports that seven laws on aging had been passed since 1959, but adds the problems facing the elderly have become more acute with the passage of time." Top priority given to Federal action on health care costs; wide array of other actions proposed. Note: "Developments" has since been published annually.

154   US Senate. Committee on Labor and Public Welfare, Subcommittee on Problems of the Aged and Aging. (1961). Action for the Aged and Aging. SuDoc Y4.L11/2:Ag4/2. 303p.
Public policy needs modification, it is declared, in a society that sees "more and more persons living to see their own children become grandparents," and in which "we have witnessed an increase by 1 million [in the prior decade] in the number of women who have become elderly widows, with no increase in the number of men who have become elderly widowers." Top priority given to recommendations on health financing.

155   US Senate. Committee on Labor and Public Welfare, Subcommittee on Problems of the Aged and Aging. (1960). The Aged and Aging in the United States: A National Problem. SuDoc Y4.L11/2:Ag3/7. 333p.
A breakthrough report by the first Congressional unit specifically mandated to examine "the present role of the Federal Government in dealing with the problems of the aged." Emphasizes need for unified approach on health, but deals with a gamut of other subjects including: employment, income, housing, nursing homes, social services, educational needs. Historically significant appendices.

156   Van Tassel, D.; Stearns, P.N. (Eds.). (1986). Old age in a bureaucratic society: The elderly, the experts, and the state in American history. New York: Greenwood Press, 259p.
Valuable views of aging policy in the context of old age history, by authors with

varying viewpoints. A critique by Brian Gratton of new interpretations of historical influences on the elderly is informative and accompanied by excellent references. Other authors criticize old age security programs.

157   Vinyard, D. (1972). The Senate Special Committee on Aging. The Gerontolo-
      gist, 12(3), 298-303.
Reviews history, functions, and accomplishments of a United States Senate unit established in 1961 after two years of work by a predecessor subcommittee. Lacking
authority to receive and act on legislation, the Committee nevertheless is regarded
as more than a mere study group. Its role in an aging "policy system" is seen as
active, but somewhat limited.

158   Viscusi, W.K. (1979). Welfare of the elderly: An economic analysis and policy
      prescription. New York: John Wiley & Sons. 251p.
Calls for systematic rethinking of policies on aging; questions reliance on "in-kind"
government benefits or services. Acknowledges that good reasons often exist for
Federal assistance to older persons, but argues for greater balance and clearcut
goals. Example: inadequate housing programs will lead to over-reliance on expensive nursing home care.

159   Weiss, J. (Ed.). (1977). The law of the elderly. New York: Practicing Law In-
      stitute, 383p.
Directed at lawyers, this work provides insight into day-to-day practical
considerations arising in programs, including Supplemental Security Income, Social
Security (hearing procedures), disability, pension protection, Medicare, Medicaid,
protective services, and condominium conversion issues.

160   Wershow, H.J. et al. (1981). Issues of public policy: How do we best serve
      public policy? In: Wershow, H.J., (Ed.). (1981). Controversial issues in geron-
      tology. New York: Springer Publishing Company, 147-73.
Editor's commentary links essays or excerpts from guest authors on the place of
the elderly "in the post-affluent society" (I. Rosow), factors forcing rationing of
some health care (T. Arie), politics and inadequacies of Federal programs (R.
Binstock), "accountability" as an inadequate measure of a social service program
(S. Tobin and D. Thompson), and ways of broadening the tax base for social purposes (I. Wilensky). Wershow warns against hasty establishment of single-purpose
programs that take on a life of their own; nutrition program cited as example.

161   Williamson, J.B.; Shindul, J.A.; Evans, L. (1985). Aging and public policy:
      Social control or social justice? Springfield IL: Charles C. Thomas, 332p.
Traces realignment in public policy toward the elderly from a focus on questions
of social justice to questions of cost containment. Emphasizes historical perspective on policy origins, including early 19th Century shift in public support of
elderly. Three chapters criticize health policy; another asks for major restructuring
of long term care. Existing programs viewed as generally positive, but fail to
recognize wide variations of circumstances among older persons.

162   Williamson, J.B.; Evans, L.; Powell, L.A. (1982). The politics of aging: Power
      and policy. Springfield IL: Charles C. Thomas, 331p.
Focuses on political gerontology as "the study of power as it involves the elderly,"
in group and individual terms. Social Security is seen as a potent force for economic development, but one that bears the social cost of increased dependence on
government; other programs cited. "Senior power" deemed potentially influential
politically, as a loose coalition of interests.

PART TWO
SPECIFIC PROGRAMS AND ISSUES

SPECIFIC PROGRAMS AND ISSUES

INCOME AND RETIREMENT POLICY

EMPLOYMENT

163 Burkhauser, R.V.; Tolley, G.S. (1978). Older Americans and market work. The
Gerontologist, 18(5), 449-453.
A policy agenda is offered to provide more work options in later years, on the
assumption that the ending of mandatory retirement will do little by itself to keep
older Americans working. The Social Security retirement test is criticized.

164 Committee for Economic Development. (1978). Jobs for the hard-to-employ:
New directions for a public-private partnership. New York: 97p.
Expanded training and job opportunities viewed as essential for making fuller use
of the older work force. Federally assisted programs examined. The United States
Employment Service is called upon to make "a much more forceful effort to
develop improved services to employers."

165 Davis, T.F. (1980). Toward a national policy on older workers. Aging, Nos.
313-314, 12-19.
Criticizes Federal older worker policy and presents findings and proposals of the
Federal Council on Aging, on which the author served as staff economist. Recommends a Department of Labor "affirmative action program for middle-aged and
older workers."

166 Donovan, R.J. (1984). Planning for an aging work force. Aging, 343, 4-7.
A US Secretary of Labor calls for public and other actions to "assure that
our growing ranks of older citizens have opportunities to remain as productive as
possible in their later years of life." Departmental goals described.

167 Howard, E.F. (1982). Anatomy of a victory for older Americans. Perspective
on Aging, 11(5), 8-10.
A detailed account of a successful attempt to block an Administration proposal
and veto to cut off funding for a program providing part-time community service
employment for nearly 55,000 low-income older persons.

168 Kennedy, E.M. (1973). National manpower policy needed. Industrial Gerontology, Summer 1973, 1-7.
Declares that age discrimination and other difficulties persist and calls for "a
national manpower policy committed to maximize the talents and skills of middle-
aged and older workers..."

169   Kieffer, J.A. (1983). Gaining the dividends of longer life: New roles for older
       workers. Boulder CO: Westview Press, 174p.
Challenges reliance on retirement as a means of opening opportunities for younger
workers and proposes broadbased public/private strategies to promote longer working lives, including a major public service job program.

170   Levine, M. (1980). Four models for age/work policy research. The Gerontol-
       ogist, 20(5). 561-574.
Age-based generalizations to disadvantage older workers are challenged. Four
models analyze causes of the age/work effect, or employment discrimination because of age. Court decisions questioned. Exhaustive references.

171   Lichtig, A. (1982). Older unemployed suffer most. Perspective on Aging, 11(6),
       11-12, 18.
Summarizes Congressional and other data showing that unemployment for 55+
workers rose by 24 percent in 1982, as compared to 16 percent for all age groups.
Another indicator of difficulty was a 76 percent increase in age discrimination
cases filed. Corrective Congressional legislation described; social costs cited.

172   National Commission for Employment Policy. (1985). Older Workers: Prospects,
       problems and policies. NCEP Report No.17, Pt.A, 58p.
Examines the labor market position of older workers and Federal and private sector policies affecting them. Finds older workers can be successfully served by
existing public job and training programs if attention is paid to specific needs.

173   National Committee on Careers for Older Americans. (1979). Older Americans:
       An untapped resource. Washington DC: 87p.
Argues for an organized effort to make paid, self-employed, or voluntary activity
more accessible. A major goal is to overcome "unnecessary burdens" to private and
public income security programs. Part 5 gives recommendations for policy changes
and action programs by governments.

174   Ossofsky, J. (1985). Trade deficit, loss of jobs in US an "older worker prob-
       lem." Perspective on Aging, 14(5), 17-18.
Summarizes Congressional testimony stating that 5.1 million persons who lost jobs
since 1980 were 55+. The US trade deficit described as a major cause of company
closings or moves, often with severe pension losses. A National Council on the
Aging legislative agenda for displaced workers is presented.

175   Ragan, P.K.; Davis, W.J. (1981). Employment and retirement. In: Davis, R.H.
       (Ed.). Aging: Prospects and issues, Third edition. Los Angeles: The University
       of Southern California Press. 288-296.
Asks greater investment in research knowledge base on older worker and retirement issues. Greater attention urged to new means of continuing full-time work or
providing the part-time option.

176   Ragan, P.K. (Ed.). (1980). Work and retirement: Policy issues. Los Angeles:
       The University of Southern California Press, 178p.

Authors examine theme that "the work/retirement sequence may well be the crucial factor in understanding what it means to be old in this society." Governmental
roles in adjusting to new employment patterns and pension and retirement policy
examined.

177 **Robinson, P.K.; Coberly, S.; Paul, C.E. (1985). Work and retirement. In:
Binstock, R.H.; Shanas, E. (Eds.). Handbook of aging and the social sciences.
New York: Van Nostrand Reinhold Company, 503–527.**
Summarizes factors contributing to continuing decline of workforce participation
among older workers at a time when economic and social factors would seem to
dictate greater participation. Relates the early retirement decision to policy
issues. Data gaps cited. Employers' viewpoint considered.

178 **Rother, J.; Edwards, C. (1982). Federal policy can no longer neglect older
workers. Generations, 6(4), 16–17, 69.**
Notes that the interest of older workers in alternative work patterns coincides
with interests of other groups, including working mothers and part-time students.
Proposes changes in retirement, employment, education policy.

179 **Shatto, G.M. (Ed.). (1972). Employment of the middle-aged. Springfield, IL:
Charles C. Thomas, 209p.**
Governmental encouragement for the middle-aged is discussed in the final three
chapters. Theodor Schuchat traces stages of legislative action. Ian Campbell reports on older worker programs in Canada. Charles E. Odell describes Federal programs for the middle-aged then available.

180 **Sommers, T.L. (1976). A free-lance agitator confronts the establishment. In:
Gross, R.; Gross, B.; Seidman, S. The new old: Struggling for decent aging.
Garden City NY: Anchor Books. 231–40.**
Blocks to employment opportunity of older persons seen as promoting dependency,
notably the Social Security retirement test. Less obvious are health care and pension plans that raise costs for 55+ persons. Broadened job openings in public programs, without exploitation, proposed.

181 **US Congress. Office of Technology Assessment. (1985). Workplace technology
and the employment of older adults. In: Technology and aging in America.
Washington DC: OTA-BA-264, 335–366.**
Maturing of the labor force expected to cause a need to use technology for
retraining and possibly for assistive devices to compensate for functional losses.
Federal policy options listed. Technical memos on assistive devices, other topics.

182 **US Senate. Special Committee on Aging. (1980). Emerging options for work
and retirement policy. SuDoc Y4,Ag4:W89, 186p.**
Offers extensive policy options affecting the employment, income, and retirement
practices of older Americans. Major headings: benefit adequacy and fairness,
financial issues related to retirement systems and pension plans, employment issues,
and system coordination.

PRIVATE PENSIONS

183 Ippolito, R.A. (1986). Pensions, economics, and public policy. Homewood, IL,
     Dow Jones-Irwin (for Pension Research Council, Wharton School, University of
     Pennsylvania), 264p.
Draws upon 1980-4 research at US Department of Labor to argue for public policy
changes intended to eliminate "artificial obstacles to voluntary market solutions for
generating retirement income." Urges greater use of individual retirement accounts
and "privatized" Federal pension insurance.

184 King, F.P. (1982). Indexing retirement benefits. The Gerontologist, 22(6),
     488-497.
Contrasts indexing of Social Security and governmental pension benefits to private
pension plan practices. Full indexing of benefits to changes in the consumer price
index is limited largely to plans established and administered by the Federal Government.

185 Rifkin, J.; Barber, R. (1978). The north will rise again: Pensions, politics, and
     power in the 1980s. Boston: Beacon Press, 279p.
Asserts that pension funds are financing runaway shops and anti-union employers
and argues for the rank-and-file union members to have a voice in fund investment
designed to serve social purposes. Chapter 21 discusses ways in which state-union
alliances can meet Federal prudence standards.

186 Schieber, S.J. (1982). Trends in pension coverage and benefit receipt. The
     Gerontologist, 22(6), 474-481.
Challenges predictions that pension growth stagnation would continue in foresee-
able future. Foresees enhancement of income security of many future retirees even
though average benefit per recipient may not increase significantly. Simulation
model weighs potential effects of possible policy changes.

187 Schiller, B.R.; Snyder, D.C. (1982). Restrictive pension provisions and the
     older worker. The Gerontologist, 22(6), 482-487.
Identifies and discusses seven pension provisions that, separately or in conjunction
with one another, limit older worker employment opportunities. At a time when
many policymakers wish to delay retirement age to reduce pressure on Social
Security, such restrictions may pose dilemmas to older workers.

188 Schulz, J.H. (1981). Pension policy at a crossroads: What should be the pen-
     sion mix? The Gerontologist, 21(1), 46-53.
To work towards an integrated policy, the author recommends: liberalizing Social
Security by improving women's benefits and targeting other reforms directed at the
most vulnerable, broadening Social Security revenues, and promoting realistic integration provisions for Social Security and private pensions.

189 Tracy, M.B; Ward, R.L. (1986). Trends in old-age pensions for women:
     Benefit levels in 10 nations, 1960-1980. The Gerontologist, 26(3), 286-291.
Women's benefits are determined to fall behind men's in 5 of nations studied. In
the United States, the benefit level of women's old age pensions is proportionately
lower than in any of the other study countries: Australia, Finland, France,
Germany, Netherlands, New Zealand, Sweden, Switzerland, and the United Kingdom.

190   US General Accounting Office. (1983). Legislative changes needed to finan-
       cially strengthen single employer pension plan insurance program. GAO/HRD-
       84-5, 73p.
Steps proposed to strengthen financial position of the Pension Benefit Guaranty
Corporation single-employer termination insurance program. Increases in premiums
requested. Describes almost ten years of regulation under the 1974 Employee
Retirement Income Security Act and its goals for private pensions.

191   US Senate. Special Committee on Aging. (1986). The cost of mandating pen-
       sion accruals for older workers. SuDoc Y4.Ag4:S.Prt.99-133, 61p.
Addresses problem of employers' ceasing pension contributions and credits for
active employees who work beyond the normal retirement age specified in company
plans (usually age 65). Finds that requiring continued pension contributions would
not significantly affect total US pension costs.

RETIREMENT INCOME

192   Beattie, W.M. (1983). Economic security for the elderly: National and inter-
       national perspectives. The Gerontologist, 23(4), 406-410.
Challenges "laissez-faire incrementalism" and asks for radical, broadbased change in
formulating retirement income policy. A new "lifespan and intergenerational
approach" would link employment goals for the young with future needs in old age;
high priority would be given to inequities facing women.

193   Binstock, R.H. (1981). A policy framework for eliminating poverty among the
       aged. Brandeis University, MA: National Aging Policy Center on Income Main-
       tenance, 15p.
Argues for replacement of the Supplemental Security Income program and Social
Security Old Age and Survivors Insurance with a guaranteed annual minimum income raising benefits above the poverty level, possibly at less cost than present
programs.

194   Borzilleri, T.C. (1980). In kind benefit programs and retirement income ade-
       quacy. Washington DC: Retirement Income: Who gets how much and who
       pays? A National Journal Issues Book. 34-38.
Noncash Federal benefits can significantly improve circumstances of older persons.
This analysis warns against pitfalls in imputing dollar values to such benefits, but
provides one methodology for arriving at a rough measure. Forty to 45 percent of
incomes below $5,000 may be provided by such programs.

195   Borzilleri, T.C. (1978) The need for a separate consumer price index for old-
       er persons: A review and new evidence. The Gerontologist, 18(3), 230-236.
A 1972 law indexed Social Security benefits according to the Consumer Price
Index. This article examines arguments for a separate older persons' CPI and finds,
from examination of 1972-1973 consumer expenditure surveys, that prices increased
approximately 4 percent faster for older people than reflected in CPI.

196   Clark, R.L.; Baumer, D.L. (1985). Income maintenance policies. In: Binstock,
       R.H.; Shanas, E. (Eds.). Handbook of aging and the social sciences. New York:
       Van Nostrand Reinhold Company, 666-695.
An informative, comprehensive review, concluding that the United States and most
developed nations face the prospect of significant future tax increases or benefit
reductions because of continued population aging. Fundamental changes in such
programs is expected within five years. Policy options discussed.

197   Clark, R.L.; Sumner, D.A. (1985). Inflation and the real income of the
      elderly: Recent evidence and expectations for the future. The Gerontologist,
      25(2), 146-152.
Rejects hypothesis that elderly are more vulnerable to inflation than other age
groups. Reports that 86 Federal programs in 1981 increased benefits based on
varying indices. Changes in methods of indexing Social Security and other programs
are discussed.

198   Greenough, W.C.; King, F.P. (1976). Pension plans and public policy. New
      York: Columbia University Press, 311p.
Examines in depth "the three major components of our old-age income support
structure: Social Security, private pensions, and public employee pensions." Its
early appraisal of the 1974 Employee Retirement Income Security Act declares
that Act began a new period of maturity for the private pension system.

199   Grimaldi, P.L. (1982). Measured inflation and the elderly. 1973-1981. The
      Gerontologist, 22(4), 347-353.
Questions widely held belief that elderly inflation rates are higher than the
general population, and that a price index for the elderly would measure their
inflation rates more accurately. Targeted assistance payments favored over general
Social Security rise to close gaps for poor.

200   Habib, J. (1985). The economy and the aged. In: Binstock, R.H.; Shanas, E.
      (Eds.). Handbook of aging and the social sciences. New York: Van Nostrand
      Reinhold Company, 479-502.
Urges policymakers to take a broad view of retirement income policy going beyond
actuarial projections for individual programs. Summarizes influences of such factors
as private consumption, investment trends, Social Security contribution rates, the
government deficit, and intergenerational transfers.

201   Herzog, B.R. (1978). Providing income and opportunities for work: Future
      policy changes. In: Herzog, B.R. (Ed.). Aging and income: Programs and
      prospects for the elderly. New York: Human Sciences Press, 309-341.
Reviews social and economic factors likely to force a new receptivity "to the
option of creating more opportunity and incentive for older people to remain in
the work force." The prospect of continued chances for work is viewed as likely
to foster positive attitudes toward the aging process.

202   Kreps, J. (1978). The economics of aging. In: Gross, R.; Gross, B.; Seidman,
      S. The new old: Struggling for decent aging. Garden City NY: Anchor Books.
      66-73.
Takes lifetime perspective on chances for accumulating retirement security, and
concludes that earnings peaks and valleys must be smoothed. Offers policy options
and relates them to potential individual choices. Retiming of consumption for the
low-income, however, is unlikely.

203   March, M.S. (1981). An analysis of the development and rationales of the
      United States income security system. US House of Representatives. Select
      Committee on Aging: SuDoc Y4:Ag4/2:In2/5.
A survey of "some of the various social and economic conditions and philosophic
rationales which have led to the development of certain public and private income
security programs." Useful insights and comparisons.

204 Moon, M. (1986). Impact of the Reagan years on the distribution of income of the elderly. The Gerontologist, 26(1), 32-37.
Social Security, indexed for inflation, viewed as essential stabilizing retirement income factor through 1980-4, despite cost-of-living payment lag in 1983. Author warns that further reduction of benefits would have especially adverse impacts on lowest-income elders.

205 Morrison, M.H. (1982). (Ed.). Economics of aging: The future of retirement. New York: Van Nostrand Reinhold, 294p.
An informative compilation giving extensive attention to long-term financing of retirement benefits and present and potential sources of retirement income.

206 Morrison, M.H. (1976). Planning for income adequacy in retirement: The expectations of current workers. The Gerontologist, 16(6), 538-543.
Findings from a survey of 588 employees show substantial knowledge gaps of retirement income needs. Though tentative, the data challenge the assumption of some policymakers "that personal savings are or will be an important component in maintaining income adequacy in retirement."

207 Myles, J. (1984). Old age in the welfare state: The political economy of public pensions. Boston: Little, Brown and Company, 140p.
Examines principles underlying considerable variations in pension practices of contemporary capitalist democracies, with frequent references to programs in the United States. Provides historical, comparative analyses.

208 President's Commission on Pension Policy. (1981). Coming of age: Toward a national retirement income policy. Washington DC: 130p.
Declares "a crisis exists in our retirement income programs" and proposes "long-term shifting of dependency on pay-as-you-go financed Federal programs such as Social Security, welfare, and in-kind benefit programs to a balanced program of employee pensions, Social Security and individual effort."

209 Schulz, J.H. (1985). Economics of aging, (Third edition). Belmont CA: Wadsworth Publishing Company, 212p.
A sophisticated synthesis of public and private factors affecting retirement economic security. Includes analysis of historic 1983 Social Security amendments and future options. Private pensions called a major, but largely neglected, area for national attention.

210 Schulz, J.H. (1985). To old folks with love: Aged income maintenance in America. The Gerontologist, 25(5), 464-71.
Social Security viewed as a touchstone--assuring stability of benefits and dignity for beneficiaries--developed by a "longstanding liberal-conservative consensus to rely almost exclusively on payroll taxes." Social Security alone, however, likely to be inadequate; a "mix" of public and private pensions is needed.

211 Schulz, J.H. (1982). Inflation's challenge to aged income security. The Gerontologist, 22(2), 115-116.
Full indexing of Social Security, Supplemental Security Income, Federal pensions and food stamp benefits provides important protection. The near-poor aged, however, are most vulnerable to inflation. Government policy shifts could make private pensions more helpful.

212   Schulz, J.H. (1974). Reform in the United States. In: Schulz, J.H., et al. Providing adequate retirement income: Pension reform in the United States and abroad. Hanover NH: University Press of New England. 221-267.
Draws upon comparisons of the United States public and private pension system with those of Sweden, Federal Republic of Germany, Belgium, and Canada. Methods of measuring adequacy by earnings replacement discussed. Outstanding bibliographies.

213   US Congress. Joint Economic Committee. (1967). Old age income assurance, Parts 1-6. Joint Committee Print. 1300p.
A compendium of papers on general policy guidelines, the aged population and retirement income programs, other public programs, employment aspects of pension plans, and financial aspects of pension plans. Volume six gives abstracts of the papers. Historically significant diversity of opinion.

214   US Senate. Special Committee on Aging. (1970). Economics of aging: Toward a full share in abundance. S.Report 91-1548. 222p.
The final document in an exhaustive study notable not only for its close inspection of sources of retirement income, but also for its consideration of health, housing, and employment aspects of economic security. Helped make the case for sweeping 1972 Social Security amendments.

RETIREMENT POLICY

215   Aaron, H.J.; Burtless, G. (Eds.). (1984). Retirement and economic behavior. Washington DC: The Brookings Institution, 332p.
Includes projections of retirement incomes in the next century and the policy changes needed to accommodate them. Changes in labor supply and demands are factored into varying views of the future. An effort has been made to make technical data and findings useful to lay readers.

216   Bradley, T.E. (1977). Alternatives to mandatory retirement. Perspective on Aging, 6(5), 12-16.
A useful summation of arguments made during the successful Congressional effort to reduce ill effects of forced retirement. Suggestions made for new Department of Labor initiatives to reduce age discrimination in employment and for Congressional action to encourage flexible older worker policies.

217   Calhoun, R.B. (1978). Building a retirement ethic, 1945-1970. In: Calhoun, R.B. In search of the new old: Redefining old age in America: 1945-1970. New York: Elsevier, 35-66.
Informative account of impetus provided to mass retirement at a fixed age by public policy—most notably the Social Security Act of 1935 and tax incentives beginning in 1926—and "irresistible" pressures for private pensions generated by organized labor and the desire of management to control labor force size.

218   Campbell, S. (1979). Delayed mandatory retirement and the working women. The Gerontologist, 19(3), 257-263.
Discussion of 1978 legislation having the effect of raising mandatory retirement age from 65 to 70 is usually focused on male workers, yet the long range effects on women workers may be at least equally profound. One effect may be more flexibility for women whose careers began in middle life.

219   Cantrell, R.S.; Clark, R.L. (1980). Retirement policy and promotional aspects. The Gerontologist, 20(5), 575-580.
Age Discrimination Act amendments in 1978 prohibited job bias because of age until age 70. Authors use an age structure model to determine that raising mandatory retirement age will retard the rate of promotion prospects only slightly, except for certain top positions and firms.

220   Fields, G.S.; Mitchell, O.S. (1984). Retirement, pensions, and Social Security. Cambridge MA: The MIT Press, 152p.
Offers empirical evidence on factors related to individual retirement decisions on a life cycle basis. Relationships of earnings, private pension and Social Security as affected by health, expectations, and other noneconomic factors examined. 1983 Social Security amendments briefly discussed.

221   Fillenbaum, G.C.; George, L.K.; Palmore, E.B. (1985). Determinants and consequences of retirement among men of different races and economic levels. Journal of Gerontology, 40(1), 85-94.
Concern expressed about current policies "which support those at the ends of the economic spectrum" but which give little assistance to the "marginal man" who must rely on enforced saving and limited pension income. Increased availability of portable pensions recommended.

222   Foner, A.; Schwab, K. (1981). Aging and retirement. Monterey CA: Brooks/ Cole Publishing Co., 132p.
A good review of retirement from a personal viewpoint, affected by push-pull societal policy and practices. Private and public agendas often do not mesh. Policy alterations in a changing society, early retirement trend discussed.

223   Graebner, W. (1980). A history of retirement: The meaning and function of an American institution, 1885-1978. New Haven CT: Yale University Press, 298p.
A well-documented study illuminating interplay between private employment practices, public policy, and the expectations of individual workers. Chapter 9, "The Reconsideration of Retirement: The 1970s", gives valuable information on legislative and other changes.

224   Lester, R.A. (1981). Age, performance, and retirement legislation. In: Somers, A.R.; Fabian, D.R. (Eds.) The geriatric imperative: An introduction to gerontology and clinical geriatrics. New York, Appleton-Century-Crofts, 77-87.
Examines exemptions provided in the 1978 amendments to the Age Discrimination Act for tenured university faculty members and key business executives. Concludes that the executive exemption should be continued without change and that the faculty exemption should be extended, preferably for an indefinite period.

225   Morrison, M.H. (1986). Work and retirement in an older society. In: Pifer, A.; Bronte, L. (Eds.). Our aging society: Paradox and promise. New York: W.W. Norton, 341-365.
Tomorrow's social imperative is a new concept of retirement, or "the acknowledgement of a productive life stage between middle and older age." Author argues for a social consensus based upon re-examination of current attitudes and practices. Valuable perspective on evolution of retirement policy.

226   Morrison, M.H. (1983). Health circumstances a major factor in the retirement decision. Aging and Work, 6(2), 89-92.
Reviews studies suggesting that serious health impairments are a major reason for early retirement and claims for reduced public benefits. Note: This article and four others in the same issue focus on a dispute on extent of disability and collection of benefits.

227   Palmore, E.B. (1972). Compulsory versus flexible retirement: Issues and facts. The Gerontologist, 12(4), 343-348.
Finds that compulsory retirement policies affected about half of the male wage and salary workers retiring at age 65. Gives arguments for and against forced retirement; offers proposals for flexible retirement including removal of the age limit then in effect in the Age Discrimination in Employment law.

228   Quinn, J.F. (1981). The extent and correlates of partial retirement. The Gerontologist, 21(6), 634-643.
Analysis of the longitudinal Retirement History Study (1969-1979) shows that partial retirement predominated for the self-employed, while only 5 percent of wage and salary respondents considered themselves so. Author suggests that part-time arrangements would reduce demands on Social Security.

229   Rix, S.E.; Fisher, P. (1982). Retirement-age policy: An international perspective. New York: Pergamon Press, 144p.
A timely analysis of differences between the United States and Denmark, France, Sweden, West Germany and the United Kingdom in accommodating demand for adequate public pensions in the face of growing demand and a strong early retirement trend. Discusses European efforts to make part-time work more generally available.

230   Sheppard, H.L. (1978). The mandatory retirement issue. In: The Annals of the American Academy of Political and Social Science. 438 (July). 40-49.
A then-new Federal statute providing anti-discrimination protection up to age 70 is examined; anticipated effects described as modest, but the mandatory retirement issue may persist as a constitutional issue. Research questions posed; economic impact of early retirement discussed.

231   Sheppard, H.L.; Rix, S.E. (1977). The graying of working America: The coming crisis in retirement-age policy. New York: The Free Press, 174p.
Asks for a re-examination of retirement policy in light of significant trends, notably the fact that more and more persons are retiring at earlier and earlier ages. Problems of changing retirement age acknowledged, but widespread change foreseen before 2,000. Similar need seen in other nations.

232   Streib, G.F.; Schneider, C.J. (1971). Retirement in American society: Impact and process. Ithaca NY: Cornell University Press, 316p.
An account of the landmark Cornell Study of Occupational Retirement, providing findings helpful to shapers of retirement policy. Almost 2,000 subjects in interviews spanning seven years provide facts refuting common stereotypes. Authors advance a "differential disengagement" conceptualization.

233   US General Accounting Office. (1978). Inconsistencies in retirement age: Issues and implications. 45p.

A useful compilation of many of the issues and problems associated with retirement age trends and future impacts, with special emphasis upon the continuing trend to early retirement in Federal and private retirement programs.

SOCIAL SECURITY

234   Achenbaum, A. (1986). The elderly's Social Security entitlements as a measure of modern American life. In: Van Tassel, D.; Stearns, P.N. (Eds.). Old age in a bureaucratic society: The elderly, the experts, and the state in American history. New York: Greenwood Press, 156-92.
Political and historical factors in the evolution of Social Security explored; need seen for questioning of common, often mistaken assumptions about fundamental principles and "a persistent failure to recognize the incongruity between entitlements and expectations." Informative notes.

235   Ball, R.E. (1978). Social Security today and tomorrow. New York: Columbia University Press, 528p.
A definitive sourcebook on the "new" Social Security system that emerged from extensive legislation in the 1970s, with special attention to fundamental principles. Traces relationships of retirement, disability, survivors, and Medicare components. "Program for future" proposed. Selected bibliography.

236   Booth, P. (1973). Social Security in America. Ann Arbor MI: University of Michigan Institute of Labor and Industrial Relations, 179p.
Casts a wide net covering Federal, Federal-State, and employer measures dealing with "the contingencies of retirement, invalidity, survivorship, unemployment, and disability, as well as health insurance." Especially strong on program evolution; good treatment of partial successes in disability protection.

237   Brodsky, D.M. (1983). Raising the Social Security retirement age: A political economy perspective. Aging and Work, 6(2), 141-150p.
A balanced presentation, made before the 1983 Social Security amendments that will gradually raise eligibility age. Foresees benefits to the system, but warns that upward adjustments "will come at the expense of future retirees and against the expressed preferences of the American public."

238   Brown, J.D. (1972). An American philosophy of Social Security: Evolution and issues. Princeton University Press, 244p.
A lucid account of the evolution of Social Security system by one of the leaders in its design and development. Describes the malleable concept of a "three-layer approach" with social insurance bracketed by needs-tested public assistance and private pensions.

239   Burkhauser, R.V.; Holden, K.C. (Eds.). (1982). A challenge to Social security: The changing roles of women and men in American society. New York: Academic Press, 272p.
Women (and many men in nontraditional roles) face inequitable treatment under Social Security; editors' introduction challenges view that spouse and survivors' benefits are solely women's issues. Contributing authors deal with earnings sharing by spouses, disability insurance, and standards for income adequacy.

240   Burton, J.L. (1980). Elder women suffer frequently and severely during retirement. Generations, 4(4), 12, 36.

A brisk but informative account, by the Chairman of the Subcommittee on Retirement Income of the House Select Committee on Aging, on growing Congressional
recognition of Social Security disparities affecting women, and examples of corrective legislation then under consideration.

241   Campbell, C.D. (Ed.). (1984). Controlling the cost of Social Security. Lexington MA: Lexington Books, 269p.

A compilation of papers presented at an American Enterprise Institute Conference.
Five of eight chapters were written by economists suggesting varying ways to
strengthen system financing. Women's issues receive extensive attention.

242   Carlson, E. (1984). Social Security fix: A look at what lies ahead. Modern
Maturity, 27(4), 28-38.

Calls the 1983 Social Security amendments a "political tour de force" with far-
reaching consequences. Pinpoints benefits lost in the compromise; warns that Medicare is confronted by even more complex difficulties.

243   Clement, P.F. (1985). History of US aged's poverty shows welfare program
changes. Perspective on Aging, 9(2), 20-23.

A history, from the colonial era to the present, of efforts to assist the indigent
aged, and the frequent disruptions of such assistance. Social Security regarded as
the most effective anti-poverty program, subject to fewer shocks than welfare
programs that assist only the poor.

244   Cohen, W.; Ball, R. (Eds.). (1985). Report of the Committee on Economic
Security of 1935: And other basic documents relating to the development of
the Social Security Act. Washington DC: National Conference on Social Welfare, 188p.

A useful compilation including legislation from 1935-1939, Supreme Court decisions,
and background studies. The editors, long associated with the evolution of Social
Security, offer commentary and perspective.

245   Cohen, W.; Friedman, M. (1972.). Social Security: Universal or selective?
Washington DC: American Enterprise Institute, 114p.

In debate format, an architect of Social Security and a prominent economist argue
their positions at a critical time in the development of social insurance in the
United States. Cohen analyzes underlying principles. Friedman concludes that "the
present system cannot be justified."

246   Derthick, M. (1981). How easy votes on Social Security came to an end. In:
Hudson, R.B. (Ed.). The aging in politics: Process and policy. Springfield IL:
Charles C. Thomas, 151-161. (Reprinted from: The Public Interest, Winter,
1979.)

Social Security financing problems of the 1970s said to have been caused by factors beyond the economic slowdown, as the system approached maturity and new
indexing features reduced room for maneuvering. Future options will alter worker
attitudes. A "massive deficit" in public understanding hinders improvement.

247 Derthick, M. (1979). Policymaking for Social Security. Washington DC: The
     Urban Institute, 446p.
A detailed account of the roles played by government professionals, members of
Congress, and eminent experts in private life in shaping and implementing programs
grouped under social insurance heading. Warns that the disability and Supplemental
Security Income programs may cause severe tests of the system.

248 Estes, C.L. (1983). Social Security: the social construction of a crisis. Mil-
     bank Memorial Fund Quarterly. 61(3), 451-461.
On the eve of 1983 Social Security legislation, it is argued that a "delegitimation"
process was blaming the elderly for the system's funding problems. The construction of crisis occurs "as a consequence of social perception and definition."

249 Ferrara, P.J. (1983). The prospect of real reform. Cato Journal,3(2), 609-620.
     Rejects the 1983 Social Security amendments as a "rescue plan that hurts
everyone" but that "hardly even adresses the fundamental problems..." Suggests a
broadened Individual Retirement Account program, other changes.

250 Forman, M. (1985). Social Security is a women's issue. In: Hess, B.B.;
     Markson, E.W. (Eds.). Growing old in America: New perspectives on old age.
     New Brunswick NJ: Transaction Books, 547-562.
Analyzes 1983 Social Security amendments and finds that positive provisions were
overshadowed by actions still needed to give women greater protection. The law
failed to recognize marriage as a partnership or provide women with greater port-
ability of coverage.

251 Gordon, M.S. (1970). Aging and income security in the United States:
     Thirty-five years after the Social Security Act. The Gerontologist, 10(4), Pt
     II, 23-31.
A useful analysis, at a turning point for Social Security, proposing adoption of a
guaranteed minimum income with negative income tax features for the entire population (instead of the Supplemental Security Income program enacted three years
later). Adequate social insurance programs seen as also essential.

252 Gwirtzman, M. (1985). Social Security into terra incognita. Journal of the
     Institute for Socioeconomic Studies, 10(3), 513-536.
Asserts that Congressional disputes in the 1980s over full, partial, or no cost-of-
living adjustments (COLAs) under Social Security have raised the question of
whether automatic COLAs should be replaced with legislative deliberations taking
the state of economy, people's needs, and the deficit into consideration.

253 Holden, K.C. (1979). The inequitable distribution of OASI benefits among
     homemakers. The Gerontologist, 19(3), 250-256.
Supplemental spouse benefits under Old Age and Survivors Insurance regarded as an
implicit homemaker's credit, but wide variations in the amount of that credit exist
because it is geared to the size of the husband's benefit. A call is made for an
explicit policy decision to put a clearcut value upon homework.

254 Hollister, R. (1974). Social mythology and reform: Income maintenance for the
     aged. In: Eisele, F.R. (Ed.). The political consequences of aging. The Annals
     of the American Academy of Political and Social Science. 415(Sept), 19-40.

Questions the argument that Social Security is analogous to private insurance. Citing 1972 amendments that raised payroll taxes and established the Supplemental Security Income Program, author predicts that income redistribution features of Social Security will become redundant and subject to criticism.

255   Kahne, H. (1981). Women and Social Security: Social policy adjusts to social change. International Journal of Aging and Human Development, 13(3), 195-208.
Social Security is often drastically inadequate for women, partially because of an "unfortunate disjunction between the assumptions upon which present Social Security provisions are based and the contemporary roles and lifetime living patterns of women." Immediate and long-term reforms proposed.

256   Kaplan, B. (1985). Social Security 50 years later. Perspective on Aging, 9(2). 4-7,28.
The political environment of Social Security in the 1980s is portrayed as one of simplistic concern about the "graying of the budget" while ignoring positive developments including the growth of the Social Security Trust Fund because of long-range action taken in 1983 amendments.

257   Kingson, E.R. (1983). Social Security and you: What's new, what's true. New York: World Almanac Publications, 95p.
Social Security called "an essential American institution." Retirement survivors, disability, and Medicare benefits described in detail, as are provisions of the compromise 1983 amendments designed to maintain financial soundness of system for decades to come. "Future issues" include general revenues use.

258   Kreps, J. (1980). Social security in the coming decade: Questions for a mature system. In: Monk, A. (Ed.). The age of aging: A reader in social gerontology. Buffalo NY: Prometheus Books, 328-343. (Reprinted from Social Security Bulletin, March 1976.)
Questions confronting Social Security in an advanced state of its development include: much higher costs for more substantial benefits, the growing population to be supported, and funding's impact on society and the economy.

259   Munnell, A.H. (1985). Social Security and the budget. New England Economic Review, July/August, 5-18.
Reports that the traditional way of measuring the impact of Social Security trust funds on the unified budget deficit has significantly understated the amount by which these programs have reduced the Treasury's required private borrowing. Good technical appendix.

260   Munnell, A.H. (1977). The future of Social Security. Washington DC: The Brookings Institution, 190p.
Focuses on Old Age and Survivors Insurance, rather than entire Social Security system. Questions whether payroll tax can provide sufficient financing and detects an "ambivalence of goals" in a system combining social insurance and welfare goals. Appendix provides good legislative history.

261   Myers, R.J. (1985). Social Security. (Third edition). Bryn Mawr PA: McCahan Foundation, 925p.

Social Security is analyzed by key components including Old Age, Survivors and Disability Insurance, Medicare, public assistance, railroad retirement, and unemployment insurance. Underlying concepts of each are summarized; foreign systems discussed. Valuable appendices, bibliography.

262   Myles, J. (1985). The trillion-dollar misunderstanding. In: Hess, B.B.; Markson, E.W. (Eds.). Growing old in America: New perspectives in old age. New Brunswick NJ: Transaction Books, 507-523.
Argues that proposed cuts of Social Security in 1981 were the "culmination of conservative assaults... spanning a decade." Those who attack the system fail to "offer a remedy that serves the need of retired people." New debate, free of purely ideological focus, seen as needed.

263   National Center for Policy Analysis. (1983). The effect of the Social Security system on black Americans. Washington DC: 13p.
Reports that lower life expectancy at birth is a key reason for blacks to be "over-represented among the taxpayers and under-represented among the beneficiaries."

264   National Commission on Social Security. (1981). Social Security in America's future. Washington DC. 414p.
An independent body of private citizens, reporting directly to the President and Congress under authority of a 1977 statute, concludes a two-year study with a fundamental finding that the Social Security system is sound and the best structure for the United States. Offers many financing recommendations.

265   National Commission on Social Security Reform. (1983). Final Report. 200p.
       Established in 1981, a 15-member body charged with reviewing "relevant analyses of the current and long-term financial condition of the Social Security trust funds," two years later offered this report, largely adopted in sweeping compromise legislation enacted later in 1983. Essential system principles supported.

266   Ozawa, M.N. (1982). Who receives subsidies through Social Security, and how much? Social Work, 27(2), 129-134.
Examines late data to determine how much of current retiree benefits are paid by past contributions plus interest. Finds a higher return than private annuities. Suggests modifications for greater equity to low-income persons.

267   Quadagno, J.S. (1986). The transformation of old age security. In: Van Tassel, D.; Stearns, P.N. (Eds.). Old age in a bureaucratic society: The elderly, the experts, and the state in American history. New York: Greenwood Press, 129-155.
Traces economic assistance for the elderly in the broader context of the history of relief from colonial times. Social Security described as a complex mixture of every social welfare device known, including 19th Century poor laws.

268   Robertson, A.H. (1983). The National Commission's failure to achieve real reform. Cato Journal, 3(2), 403-416.
Finds that the January 1983 report of the National Commission on Social Security (largely adopted in legislation soon after) was "extremely disappointing;" focused on finances rather than fundamental system "design" flaws.

269   Schieber, S.J. (1982). Social Security: Perspectives on preserving the system.
Washington DC: Employee Benefit Research Institute, 302p.
Somewhat outdated by later legislation, this far-ranging study gives useful information on the development of the system, long- and short-range financing, and
equity issues. Predicts that growth of private pensions can help relieve some of
the burden.

270   Schulz, J.H. (1978). Liberalizing the Social Security retirement test: Who
would receive the increased pension benefits? Journal of Gerontology, 33(2),
262-268.
The controversial retirement test makes payment of benefits depend on partial or
complete cessation of specified employment. The author finds that significant liberalization could occur without the benefits going primarily to the higher-income
aged. Complete abolition, however, would have the opposite effect.

271   Task Force on Social Security. (1983). Social Security: A tax on labor. Washington DC: Small Business Administration, 28p.
Attempts "to assert the voice of the entrepreneur" in the Social Security debate;
argues that small companies and employees pay disproportionately more into the
system. States that companies with 58 or fewer workers employ more than 50 percent of covered workers.

272   US House of Representatives. Select Committee on Aging. (1982). Cost of
living adjustments under the Old Age, Survivors, and Disability (Social Security) program. SuDoc Y4.Ag4/2:So1/13. 28p.
A helpful summary of the history, effects, and proposed changes in the Social
Security cost-of-living adjustments (COLA). Gives details of price indexing effects
on OASDI beneficiaries.

273   US Senate. Special Committee on Aging. (1985). Fifty years of Social Security: Past achievements and future challenges. SuDoc Y4.Ag4:S.prt.99-70. 87p.
Contributing authors focus on ambiguities in need of clarification, while recognizing enormous achievements of the system. Topics include historical perspective, intergenerational and disability issues, labor market policy, changing roles of women,
and international comparisons.

274   US Senate. Special Committee on Aging. (1982). Social Security disability:
Past, present, and future. SuDoc Y4.Ag4:So1/13. 39p.
Widespread denial and discontinuance of benefits in the early 1980s helped prompt
this review of disability insurance, its usefulness and its problems. Concern expressed about "the traumatic impact of the loss of disability benefits" and allega-
tions of improprieties in the disability examinations.

SUPPLEMENTAL SECURITY INCOME

275   Allison, G. (1975). The Supplemental Security Income program and welfare
reform. In: Osterbind, C.C. (Ed.). Social goals, social programs, and the aging.
Gainesville FL: University of Florida Center for Gerontological Studies,
70-82.
Helpful insights into the legislative turmoil over welfare reform and the pressures
leading to enactment of the SSI program as a partial solution. Author is sympa-
thetic to SSI purposes, but--at an early stage in its development--expresses concerns about practical consequences of its provisions, direction.

276   Burke, V.J.; Burke, V. (1981). Saved: Income guarantees for the aged. In: Hudson, R.B. (Ed.). The aging in politics: Process and policy. Springfield IL: Charles C. Thomas, 162-175.
An informative account of attempts at welfare reform in the early 1970s and the compromise action establishing the Supplemental Security Income program, described as "a quiet revolution" because it established a national responsibility to maintain an income floor for certain groups.

277   Lebowitz, B.D.; Dobra, J.L. (1976). Implementing an income strategy for the elderly: Studies in organizational change. International Journal of Aging and Human Development, 7(3), 255-267.
Data from the first year of a longitudinal study of implementation of the Supplemental Security Income program reveal administrative strains and some negative personnel attitudes within the Social Security Administration. Relationships of SSI to rationalization of the service system identified.

278   US Senate. Special Committee on Aging. (1984). The Supplemental Security Income program: A 10-year overview. SuDoc Y4.Ag4:S.prt.98-194. 266p.
Six comprehensive essays examine the degree to which SSI had achieved its original objectives in its first decade. Origins of the program and difficulties in implementing it are emphasized, as are SSI shortcomings in reducing poverty. A good legislative history is provided.

TAX POLICY

279   Nelson, G.W. (1983). Tax expenditures for the elderly. The Gerontologist, 23(5), 471-478.
Age-based income tax exemptions, exclusions, and credits are examined for tax relief effectiveness and other outcomes. Equity issues arise; author finds that a majority of the benefits are directed "to a small elite of individuals who are currently elderly or who will be elderly in the future."

280   Chen, Yung-Ping. (1966). Low income, early retirement, and tax policy. The Gerontologist, 6(1), 35-38.
Examines property tax relief and Federal and State exemptions for the elderly and concludes that tax adjustments give little real improvement in retirement income. Warns that an early retirement trend will cause substantial difficulties for tax concession policies.

281   Goldfarb, S. (1984). Lower your taxes: Use the dependent care tax credit for adult care expenses. Washington DC: National Women's Law Center, 10p.
An account of the limited, but important, tax credit available for working people, especially those with low incomes, who pay for the care of a disabled or aging family member.

HEALTH AND LONG TERM CARE

HEALTH CARE ETHICAL ISSUES

282   Avorn, J. (1984). Benefit and cost analysis in geriatric care: Turning age discrimination into health policy. The New England Journal of Medicine, 310(20), 1294-1301.
Explores limitations of cost-based analysis, especially when applied to geriatrics. Questions the "human capital" approach and the "lifeboat mentality" that assumes some passengers must be thrown overboard. Acknowledges that better resource allocation is needed.

283   Callahan, D. (1986). Health care in the aging society. In: Pifer, A.; Bronte, L. (Eds.). Our aging society: Paradox and promise. New York: W.W. Norton, 319-339.
Social values and economic realities are likely to clash increasingly as population aging continues. Economic standards will put elderly at sharp disadvantage unless clear ethical issues are heeded. Three aspirations for society recommended to shape new balance in meeting needs of young, old.

284   Clark, P.G. (1985). The social allocation of health care resources: Ethical dilemmas in age-group competition. The Gerontologist, 25(2) 119-125.
Cooperation and rational analysis seen as the means to develop principled policy. Changes recommended in structure of governmental programs and ways in which social and medical services meet needs of frail elderly population. A "lifespan" view of personal health needs recommended.

285   Kapp, M.B.; Pies, H.E.; Doudera, A.E. (Eds.). (1986). Legal and ethical aspects of health care for the elderly. Ann Arbor MI: Health Administration Press, University of Michigan, 323p.
Twenty-four experts on clinical medicine and nursing, health policy and administration, bioethics and law contribute chapters on diverse matters, yet strike a common theme: difficulties in making public programs responsive to individual persons. Technical issues well explained.

HEALTH CARE STRUCTURE

286   Baumgartner, L. (1961). Public health and aging. The Gerontologist, 1(4), 160-161.
Useful for tracking Federal legislation leading to Medicare and Medicaid. Author, then New York City Commissioner of Health, discusses 1960 legislation requiring states to evaluate and improve their public assistance medical care programs for the aged, calling it a clear mandate to tackle many problems.

287   Brody, S.J. (1971). Prepayment of medical services for the aged: An analysis. The Gerontologist, 11(2), 152-157.
Discusses an Administration/Congressional proposal (later enacted) to open health maintenance organizations (HMOs) to Medicare eligibles. Warns against regarding prepaid programs as a panacea, particularly for supplemental health social services. Points out that HMO experience with the aged is limited.

316 US Congress. Office of Technology Assessment. (1985). Information technology and the health of an aging population. In: Technology and aging in America. Washington DC: OTA-BA-264, 159-181.
Information technology can promote preventive behaviors and help manage chronic conditions; several studies have found the elderly highly receptive to using computers. Federal involvement with information technology and the aged called minimal; Congressional issues and options listed and discussed.

317 US Senate. Special Committee on Aging. Subcommittee on Health of the Elderly. (1963). Medical assistance for the aged: The Kerr-Mills program, 1960-1963. Committee Print. 103p.
Argues that a Federal-State welfare medical program begun only three years before "has proved at best an effective and piecemeal approach...". By documenting these shortcomings this report helped make the case for enactment of Medicare two years later.

318 Vladeck, B.C. (1985). Financing health care for the elderly in 2000: Issues, mechanisms, and directions. In: Gaitz, C.M.; Niederehe, G.; Wilson, N.L. (Eds.). Aging 2,000: Our health care destiny, Vol.II: Psychosocial and Policy Issues, New York, Springer-Verlag, 315-322.
Incisive, if brief, analysis of health system components and inadequacies, reasons for alarming increases in Medicare costs, and ways in which such costs may be met in the future. Urges integration of long term and acute care by easing of barriers among present programs and private financing.

319 Weaver, J.L. (1981). The elderly as a political community: The case for a national health policy. In: Hudson, R.B. (Ed.). The aging in politics: Process and policy. Springfield IL: Charles C. Thomas, 30-42.
Describes evolution of elderly's attitudes in support of Federal intervention to assure health care as "a response which transcends previous ideological and partisan attitudes, opposition and loyalties." Expects "a more and more clearly discernible community of interest and demands."

320 Wood, J.B.; Estes, C.L. (1986). The medicalization of community services for the elderly. San Francisco: Institute for Health and Aging, University of California, 26p.
Draws upon telephone survey data collected in 1983-4. Concludes that community-based service systems are responding to increasingly competitive environments in ways including targeting to most profitable services, absorption of nonprofit agencies by for-profit entities; and further fragmentation of services.

HEALTH PROMOTION

321 Burkhauser, R.V.; Butler, J.S.; Mitchell, J.M.; Pincus, T. (1986). Effects of arthritis on wage earnings. Journal of Gerontology, 41(2), 277-281.
Arthritis, reported to affect nearly one-quarter of the 45-64 population, is subjected to an economic model indicating that arthritis causes a yearly loss of approximately $17 billion in wage earnings for the United States. Intervention, it is asserted, would significantly increase earning capacity.

322   Filner, B.; Williams, T.F. (1981). Health promotion for the elderly: Reducing functional dependency. In: Somers, A.R.; Fabian, D.R. (Eds.). The geriatric imperative: An introduction to gerontology and clinical geriatrics. New York, Appleton-Century-Crofts, 105-116. (Adapted from chapter in Healthy People. The Surgeon General's report on health promotion and disease prevention. Washington DC: Institute of Medicine, National Academy of Sciences, 1979.)
This definitive summary of health promotion goals includes discussion of deficiencies in existing programs. Stresses nutrition and mental health, and gaps in health care service. Excellent references.

323   Gilbert, S. (1986). Healthy older people: A national public education campaign. Perspective on Aging, 15, 11-14.
Describes objectives of a program sponsored by the Office of Disease Prevention and Health Promotion, US Public Health Service, in cooperation with the US Administration on Aging. Five priority areas--exercise, nutrition, safe use of medicines, injury prevention, and smoking cessation--identified through research.

324   Minkler, M. (1983). Health promotion and elders: A critique. Generations, 7(3), 13-15, 67.
Suggests a broader recasting of health promotion to better meet older Americans' needs, including policy shifts to allow Medicare and Medicaid more leeway in reimbursing for preventive health services. Improved transportation access and greater "system centered" education also viewed as key elements.

325   Richmond, J.B. (1979). Health promotion and disease prevention in old age. Aging, Nos.295-296, 11-15.
An assessment by the US Surgeon General of the need for health and social support services to maintain maximum functional and social independence. No Public Health Service initiatives offered, but case made for "provision of a broad spectrum of services for the elderly at a single location."

326   Rubenstein, L.Z.; Josephson, K.R.; Nichol-Seamons, M.; Robbins, A.S. (1986). Comprehensive health screening of well elderly adults: An analysis of a community program. Journal of Gerontology, 41(3), 342-352.
Among those screened at a California community center for 55+ referred to physicians, and 15 percent reported receiving treatment from physicians within a month. Authors take an advocacy position for prevention programs, while acknowledging need for larger studies.

327   US Congress. Office of Technology Assessment. (1985). Health promotion/ disease prevention and nutrition in the elderly. In: Technology and aging in America. OTA-BA-264, 119-134.
Catalogues risk factors associated with diseases, accidents, and functional impairments encountered by elderly. Overriding Federal issue is regarded as the acute-care oriented reimbursement structure of Medicare/Medicaid. Research priorities suggested. Congressional options for numerous potential actions summarized.

HOME HEALTH SERVICES

328   Brickner, P.W. (1978). Home health care for the aged: How to help older people stay in their own homes and out of institutions. New York: Appleton-Century-Crofts, 306p.

Primarily a manual to assist in organization of home health programs following the hospital-based model of the Chelsea-Village Program of St. Vincent's Hospital, New York City. However, its chapters on nutrition, housing, transportation, cost analysis, cost comparisons, and funding analyze public programs.

329 Champlin, L. (1986). The home health care boom: Why are doctors left out? Geriatrics, 41(1), 103-105.
Urges greater physician participation in decision-making and tracking of hospital patients discharged to home care during a boom growth of in-home services. Cites corrective legislation and reasons for its demise.

330 Hayslip, B.; Ritter, M.L.; Oltman, R.M.; McDonnell, C. (1980). Home care services and the rural elderly. The Gerontologist, 20(2), 192-193.
Data about perceived home care needs in a Maryland County were obtained in 1977-78 from 299 older persons, who saw need for substantial additional services. Intensity of such response, however, varied among locales. Agency-oriented responses were less emphatic about need.

331 Koren, M.J. (1986). Home care—who cares? The New England Journal of Medicine, 314(14), 917-920.
Home care described as "a large, complex, and still rapidly expanding new health field that could benefit vast numbers of patients but operates, for all practical purposes, beyond the purview of physicians." Gives concise summary of conflicting program goals and argues for physicians to become patient advocates.

332 Pomeranz, W.; Rosenberg, S. (1986). Developing home health services in rural communities—an innovative solution to a thorny problem. Home Health Care Services Quarterly, 6(4), 5-10.
A little-known provision of the Rural Health Clinics Act (Public Law 95-210) is used to broaden range of services offered by mid-level practitioners. Authors believe that many rural communities can use the 1977 legislation.

333 Reif, L. (1984). Making dollars and sense of home health policy. Nursing Economics. Nov.-Dec. Vol.2, 382-388.
Analyzes contradictory policies and attitudes toward home care in 1980s. On the one hand, home health is seen as a cost-saving substitute for institutional care, and benefits from supportive legislation. On another, Federal and state restrictions are applied as the demand for home services grow.

334 Reif, L. (1981). Expansion of in-home services: Costly addition or viable strategy for managing those in need of long term care? Home Health Care Services Quarterly. 2(2), 1-3.
Authoritative editorial on reasons for contrasting views about cost-effectiveness and feasibility of more widespread, accessible home care services. Provisions of 1980 liberalizing legislation discussed, as is Massachusetts social model of home care. Author calls for a basic range of services.

335 Schlenker, R.E. (1980). Expanding home health services: Evaluation of the Federal grant program. Home Health Care Services Quarterly, 1(3), 49-64.
Summarizes an evaluation of a modest program authorized in 1975 to stimulate the growth and development of home health services. Finds from analysis of 56 grants made in 1976 that service expansion was achieved and that Visiting Nurses Associations led in success factors.

336   Starr, J. (1986). Testimony to October 1985 homemaker-home health aide hearing. Caring, 5(4), 28-30.
The director of a New York statewide coalition traces consequences of fragmented Federal financing of a range of in-home services, and gives recommendations for strong action at the national level.

337   Trager, B. (1980). Home health care and national health policy. New York: Haworth Press, 103p.
Evaluates fragmented approaches to publicly funded home health services and their consequences. Opportunities for capacity building described. Calls for placement of Federal responsibility in a central entity.

338   Trager, B. (1973). Homemaker/home health aide services in the United States. US Department of Health, Education, Welfare, SN 1726-0034, 234p.
Important analyses of the historical development of in-home services provided in chapter I, citing points of progression and causes of frustrations often caused by Federal policy anamolies, particularly in financing mandates. Chapter II provides useful comparisons with home help abroad.

339   Trager, B. (1972). Home Health Services in the United States. Washington DC: US Senate. Special Committee on Aging. SuDoc Y4.Ag4:H34/11, 147p.
An early analysis of the policy and practice problems that put home health service at serious disadvantage in the formative years of Medicare and Medicaid, together with a call for removal of barriers. Authoritative discussion of basic home health components and comparison with European services.

340   US General Accounting Office. (1982). The elderly should benefit from expanded home health care but increasing these services will not insure cost reductions. GAO IPE-83-1, 130p.
Finds tangible benefits to patients using expanded home health care services, but no reductions in nursing home or hospital use or total services costs. Identifies research needs. Reviews prior home health evaluations.

341   US General Accounting Office. (1977). Home health: The need for a national policy to better provide for the elderly. GAO HRD-78-19, 120p.
A significant attempt to compare nursing home costs with home care costs including estimated value of support services from family and friends, establishing a "break-even point" when informal services for highly impaired persons may exceed institutional costs.

342   US House of Representatives. Select Committee on Aging, Subcommittee on Health and Long Term Care. (1984). Building a long term care policy: Home health care data and implications. SuDoc Y4.Ag42:L85/5, 66p.
Reviews the subcommittee's efforts to raise policy priorities for in-home care and support, emphasizing policy anamolies and some positive accomplishments. Finds "a massive unmet need" among an estimated 5.5 million persons. Survey findings document home health care agency operations.

343   Wood, J.B. (1986). The effects of cost-containment on home health agencies. Home Health Care Services Quarterly, 6(4), 59-78.

Increased retrictiveness of Federal reimbursement policy is examined for 1983-4, when growth of the home health industry slowed. Many home health agencies "begin to change their tax status to for-profit status to enable them to negotiate rates." A growing "no care zone" in Medicaid is described.

LONG TERM CARE

344 Abdellah, F.G. (1978). Long term policy issues: Alternatives to institutional care. The Annals of the American Academy of Political and Social Science. 438 (July). 28-39.
A representative of the US Public Health Service describes "a major [Federal] effort to include home health and social services as a broad cost containment effort to prevent inappropriate institutionalization." Ongoing or completed demonstration projects are discussed. State-local partnership sought.

345 American College of Physicians, Health and Policy Committee. (1984). Long term care of the elderly. Annals of Internal Medicine, 100(May), 760-763.
A position paper emphasizing that long term care should go beyond nursing homes to offer numerous non-institutional alternatives. Total number of elderly in need of such care estimated to be 7.5 to 9 million by 1990. Reimbursement policies should enhance systems development; cost-cutting should not create new barriers.

346 Anderson, N.N. (1974). Approaches to improving the quality of long term care for older persons. The Gerontologist, 14(6), 519-524.
A frank account of the policy and organizational difficulties encountered in early efforts to develop a well-balanced community long term care system for the Minneapolis-St. Paul area. Nursing homes accountability sought; linkages among all other systems components described; advantages of a regional council cited.

347 Arling, G.; McAuley, W.J. (1983). The feasibility of public payments for family caregiving. The Gerontologist, 23(3), 300-306.
Two studies (in Virginia, West Virginia) cited to indicate that family members are heavily involved in support of impaired elderly, and that decision to institutionalize is based most often on non-financial factors. Policy and programmatic considerations arising in programs to assist such families are discussed.

348 Beall, G.T. (1984). Long term care cost crisis: Can private insurance bail us out? Perspective on Aging, 13(5), 20-23.
Improvement and expansion of private insurance seen as holding the promise "of undergirding the financial base" of long term care.

349 Bell, W.G. (1973). Community care for the elderly: An alternative to institutionalization. The Gerontologist, 13(3), 349-354.
Draws upon a field survey analyzing practices and procedures affecting impaired low-income elderly in Florida, where approximately 14 percent of older persons were likely to be functionally impaired. Argues for establishing community based noninstitutional services.

350 Benedict, R.C. (1979). Making the health care system responsive to the needs of the elderly. Aging, Nos.295-296, 25-27.
The US Commissioner of Aging sees the major role of the Administration on Aging as promoting development of a continuum of care and helping states "in moving

the existing health and social service networks toward a coordinated long term care system as well as to provide assistance for local development...".

351 Benjamin, A.E.; Lindeman, D.A.; Budetti, P.P.; Newacheck, P.W. (1984). Shifting commitments to long term care: The role of coordination. The Gerontologist, 24(6), 598-603.
Health planning agencies and Older American Act state and area agencies on aging have legislative mandates to establish coordination linkages. A survey reveals varying patterns, directly related to level of attention given to long term care by the agencies, which are urged to search out teamwork partners.

352 Birnbaum, H.; Burke, R.; Swearingen, C.; Dunlop, B. (1984). Implementing community-based long term care: Experience of New York's Long Term Home Health Care Program. The Gerontologist, 24(4), 380-386
Also known as the "Nursing Homes without Walls" program, this program emphasizes nursing and other care usually provided in a nursing home, but not room and board. This evaluation of the first three years says program features are replicable, but warns that considerable start-up time is required.

353 Bovbjerg, R.R.; Holahan, J. (1982). Medicaid in the Reagan era: Federal policy and state choices. Washington DC: Urban Institute Press. 72p.
Congress rejected broad devolution of Medicaid commitments in 1981 legislation but nevertheless encouraged states to economize by 3 percent cuts in Federal assistance. State efforts to contain costs before and after the 1981 legislation are analyzed; close attention given to nursing home reimbursements.

354 Branch, L.G.; Stuart, N.E. (1984). A 5-year history of targeting home care services to prevent institutionalization. The Gerontologist, 24(4), 387-391.
Federal and other funding sources are tapped by the Massachusetts statewide Home Care Corporation (40,000 clients in 1982). Close monitoring over five years leads to conclusion that services have been consistently targeted to persons with institutional care risk factors.

355 Brickfield, C.F. (1985). Who will pay for long-term care? Caring, 4(3), 23-26.
A useful summary of inadequacies of present public policies in protecting older persons and their families against long term care costs; argues for improved private insurance to fill in gaps, recognizing the difficulties in such a course.

356 Brody, E.M. (1985). Parent care as a normative family stress. The Gerontologist, 25(1), 19-29.
Summarizes available data indicating that well over 5 million people are involved in parent care at any given time. Public policy must do more than merely "cheering the family on"; but recent evidence points to negative Federal and state action. Authoritative references.

357 Brody, E.M. (1981). "Women in the middle" and family help to older people. The Gerontologist, 21(5), 471-480.
Women of middle age or the middle generation(s) are increasingly called upon to care for older family members, even as their work force participation rises. A "revised contract" between men and women is needed, as is "the formal support system that only social policy can create."

358 Brody, S.J. (1979). The thirty-to-one paradox: Health needs and medical solutions. In: Hubbard, J.P. (Ed.). (1979). Aging: Agenda for the eighties. Issues book. Washington DC. The National Journal, 17-20.
Examines Federally-assisted programs and concludes that "medically-oriented services expenditures to health/social service expenditures for the long term support to the elderly may be placed at 30 to 1." This tendency held likely to intensify unless specific policy changes are made. Lists funding sources.

359 Brody, S.J. (1977). Resources for long-term care in the community. In: Brody, E.M. Long term care for older people. New York: Human Sciences Press, 59-83.
One third of the elderly need health-social services, but may not find them in their home communities. This inventory of such resources, most of them directly linked to Federal programs, comments on policy shortcomings in many of them, including important linkage gaps, complexity, and confused mandates.

360 Brody, S.J.; Spivack, S.M. (1981). Long term health care planning: The state of the practice. In: Annual Review of Gerontology and Geriatrics, Vol.2. New York: Springer Publishing Company, 320-339.
Traces legislative mandates, often conflicting or inadequate, that could provide planning resources for long term care. Describes a Federal strategy of demonstration projects as contributing to a "sense of impounded policy."

361 Callahan, J.J. (1980). Many elders and families bear cost of long term care. Generations, 5(1), 8-9, 38.
An analytical summary of facts refining the frequent statement that 60 to 80 percent of long term services are provided by families, pointing to the difficulties in arriving at cost comparisons with formal services. Predicts that private costs of caregiving will continue to rise.

362 Callahan, J.J.; Wallack, S.S. (Eds.). (1981). Reforming the long term care system: Financial and organizational options. Lexington MA: Lexington Books, 261p.
Subjects six discrete financing and organizational proposals to vigorous comparative analyses by contributing authors, emphasizing potential combinations of features to meet varying circumstances and needs. Appendix A gives a useful summary of previous analyses of major reform options.

363 Cantor, M. (1983). Strain among caregivers: a study of experience in the United States. The Gerontologist, 23(6), 597-604.
Informal caregivers (N=111) in a New York City study report a wide variety of stresses, concerns, and helping relationships. Spouses probably at highest risk; offspring likely to suffer from a multiplicity of roles; friends and neighbors helpful but may require instruction. Data underscores "the danger of global solutions."

364 Cantor, M.; Little, V. (1985). Aging and social care. In: Binstock, R.H.; Shanas, E. (Eds.). Handbook of aging and the social sciences. New York: Van Nostrand Reinhold Company, 745-781.
Focuses on the provision of social supports to older people by formal organizations or by the extensive informal support networks of family, friends, and neighbors. Provides a conceptual model of social care from a systems perspective, details on availability on the amount of such assistance, and policy options.

365   Capitman, J.A. (1986). Community-based long term care models, target groups, and impacts on service use. The Gerontologist, 26(4). 389-404.
Analyzes five US Health Care Financing Administration-sponsored demonstrations testing varying forms of expanded community care. Finds only one project reduced nursing home use significantly, but that others produced valuable findings related to varying goals.

366   Capitman, J.A.; Haskins, B.; Bernstein, J. (1986). Case management approaches in coordinated community-oriented long term care demonstrations. The Gerontologist, 26(4), 398-404.
Uses findings from a national evaluation of Medicaid demonstrations to describe variations in case management for 15 projects, including five showing the relationship between case management and the costs of coordinating services.

367   Center for the Study of Social Policy. (1982). Tax subsidies for long term care of the elderly. Washington DEC, 79p.
Regards Federal tax relief for family caregivers as worthy of experimentation, but raises important considerations and lists targeting issues and policy choices involved in each. Three state laws described in detail.

368   Crossman, L.; London, C.; Barry, C. (1981). Older women caring for disabled spouses: A model for supportive services. The Gerontologist, 21(5), 464-470.
Uses experience obtained from a wives' support group in Marin County CA to argue for more widespread understanding of the growing need for respite to assist elderly caregivers. Argues for additional research on risk arising when wives care for husbands, and factors leading to institutionalization decision.

369   Diamond, L.M.; Gruenberg, L.; Morris, R.L. (1983). Elder care for the 1980s: Health and social service in one prepaid health maintenance system. The Gerontologist, 23(2), 148-153.
Summarizes studies and principles underlying the development and field testing of Social/Health Maintenance Organizations, "a system of health and services for an elderly population, including individuals in need of long term care, financed on a fixed budget basis."

370   Federal Council on the Aging. (1978). Public policy and the frail elderly. (Staff Report.) GPO 281-683/8040 1-3, 170p.
Directs priority attention to "persons, usually but not always, over the age of 75, who because of the accumulation of various continuing problems often require one or several supportive services in order to cope with daily life." Proposes to systematize aid, emphasizing assessment and case management.

371   Gottesman, L.E.; Ishizaki, B.; MacBride, S.M. (1979). Service management—plan and concept in Pennsylvania. The Gerontologist, 19(194), 379-385.
The Pennsylvania experience in making service, or case, management a statewide responsibility of area agencies on aging is described. Efforts to overcome fragmented services are traced to varying Federal requirements. Agency experience used to promulgate desirable system characteristics.

372   Greenberg, J.N.; Leutz, W.; Ervin, S.; Greenlick, M.; et al. (1985). S/HMO: The social/health maintenance organization and long term care. Generations, 9(4), 51-55.

A helpful summary of principles and prototype programs intended to test prepaid capitation systems providing a full range of acute and chronic care services. Difficulties and limitations recognized, but the experiment is called an important step toward insurable community-based long term care. Good references.

373   Harrington, C. (1985). Alternatives to nursing home care. Generations, 9(4), 43–46.
A convenient summary of initiatives undertaken, usually at the state level, despite fragmentation, restrictive public policies, and funding constraints. Public programs "have primarily addressed short-range approaches by adding to the existing pluralistic system rather than by making fundamental reform...".

374   Harrington, C.; Newcomer, R.J.; Estes, C.; and associates. (1985). Long term care and the elderly. Beverly Hills: Sage Publications, 280p.
Links long term care difficulties with unresolved policy issues in the acute care system; relates Federal deficiencies to state efforts at cost-cutting, reform, or both. Final chapter gives basic principles for developing a comprehensive long term care system. A timely and comprehensive analysis.

375   Harrington, C.; Newcomer, R. (1984). Social/Health Maintenance Organizations: A new policy option for the aged and disabled. San Francisco: Aging Health Policy Center. 31p.
An excellent, supportive summary of the potential of S/HMOs to improve access, continuity, and appropriateness of long term care with reduced costs through prepaid, group coverage with extensive benefits. Barriers to their evolution noted; but policymakers urged to give them a fair trial.

376   Hodgson, J.H.; Quinn, J.L. (1980). The impact of the Triage health care delivery system upon client morale, independent living, and the cost of care. The Gerontologist. 20(3), 364–371.
The State of Connecticut and the Federal Government began in 1974 to develop a health care delivery system providing easy access to participants, a simplified reimbursement system, and an innovative quality control mechanism. Implementation of the Triage concept regarded as replicable on broader scale.

377   Institute of Medicine. (1977). The elderly and functional dependency: A policy statement. Washington DC: National Academy of Sciences, (IOM Pub. 77-04.), 52p.
Declares "it is in the interest of society as well as the elderly individual to prevent the development of unnecessary dependency or minimize its impact once functional capacity has declined." Makes recommendations on long term care, prevention, service coordination and planning, education, and research.

378   Kahn, A.J. (1984). Long term care issue more demanding as other pressures mount. Perspective on Aging, 13(3), 13-16, 30.
Rejects incremental reform strategy and calls "for a larger vision" establishing a community personal care system offering universal coverage for social services financed partially by an income-based fee scale, personal care services funded through refundable tax credit, and a personal care network for isolates.

379   Kane, R.A. (1985). Long term care status quo untenable? What is more ideal for nation's elderly? Perspective on Aging, 14(5), 23-26.
Finds that practical services for chronically ill persons in the community are hard to find and even harder to afford, that high nursing home expenditures reflect national overemphasis on institutional care, and that "other aspects of the system seem to have failed older citizens." Suggests reform outcomes.

380   Kane, R.L.; Kane, R.A. (1985). A will and a way: What Americans can learn about long term care from Canada. Santa Monica CA: The RAND Corporation, 295p.
Reports on health/long term care policy in three provinces, finding as a common factor the universal health insurance system for hospital and medical care, to which each province has added a nonmeans-tested, long term care benefit. Advises the United States to establish a similar system and add refinements later.

381   Kane, R.L.; Kane, R.A. (1980). Alternatives to institutional care of the elderly: Beyond the dichotomy. The Gerontologist. 20(3). 249-259.
Proponents of alternatives to nursing home care sometimes claim that substitute services can be both better and cheaper. This definitive analysis questions easy assumptions. It finds contradictory expectations and outcomes in public policy support of experimental initiatives.

382   Kane, R.L.; Kane, R.A. (1976). Long term care in six countries: Implications for the United States. US Public Health Service, 197p.
United States compared to England, Scotland, Sweden, Norway, The Netherlands, and Israel. Dangers of divided response to long term care illustrated; importance of housing emphasized. Foresees that United States nursing home care will remain proprietary-dominated; proposes outcomes-based payments.

383   Kaplan, J. (1983). Planning the future of institutional care: The true costs. The Gerontologist, 23(4). 411-415.
A new approach to geriatric bed need that encompasses the level and status of health care and community human services is described. A useful table, "A Geriatric Methodological Approach to a Service Inventory," is offered.

384   LaVor, J. (1979). Long term care: A challenge to service systems. In: LaPorte, V.; Rubin, J. (Eds.). Reform and regulation in long term care. New York: Praeger, 18-64.
A comprehensive, well-defined examination of policy considerations, together with a balanced discussion of policy reform options by Federal entities, universities, state and local public agencies, and private components.

385   LaVor, J. (1979). Long term care and home health care: A challenge to service systems. Home Health Care Services Quarterly. 1(1), 19-71.
Examines "need to make our category-oriented system work to the benefit of the consumer with multiple needs." Reviews conflicts in existing programs; advances a proposal for an "Ambulatory Chronic Care Service."

386   Libow, L.S.; Caro, F.G.; Liota, M. (1974). Delivery of geriatric community care: Issues of leadership and models of delivery. The Gerontologist, 14(4), 286-292.
An early warning that failure of public officials and professionals to develop integrated supportive and care services for some 6 million functionally disabled persons in the United States is likely to assign to the private sector "leadership in this field as it has in delivering nursing home care."

387   Lupu, M. (1981). The role of an area agency: Advocacy and coordination. Generations, 5(3), p.17.
A succinct review by an area agency on aging director of the growing role by such agencies in long term care, together with a warning that the agency "should not muddy its role by delivering services that other agencies are geared to provide. Rather, it should strengthen and help develop these services."

388   Matlack, D.R. (1975). The case for geriatric day hospitals. The Gerontologist, 15(2), 109-113.
Suggests that British day hospital model—usually 20-40 patient places, attendance one to five days a week, local, dependable transportation—be adapted for the United States. Lack of funding a formidable obstacle, but potentially useful legislation described. Close relationship to day care acknowledged.

389   Meiners, M.R. (1985). An idea whose time has come: Long term care insurance. Generations, 9(4), 39-42.
Argues that policy and market developments are increasing momentum for private coverage to protect families against catastrophic costs. Cites research suggesting potential demand for such policies and traces incipient consumer interest. Need seen for more research and development. Brief but definitive references.

390   Meltzer, J.; Farrow, F.; Richman, H. (Eds.). (1981). Policy options in long term care. University of Chicago Press, 244p.
A generally informative compendium of data and potential program modifications needed to make suitable chronic care more widely available.

391   Monk, A. (1975). Organized day care for older persons fulfills social and emotional needs. Perspective on Aging, 4(3). 23-25.
Day care centers seen as a logical framework for avoiding institutionalization and promoting activity and socialization for many disabled persons. Three sources of Federal funding cited, but single comprehensive source needed. Research and support of day care briefly summarized.

392   Moon, M. (1980). Provisions of many public programs discourage family support of elderly. Generations, 5(1), 14-15, 39.
Emphasizes transfers by young and older family members, but lists disincentives for support by younger members in the Supplemental Security Income, food stamps, and Medicaid programs. Changes in means-testing and tax policies discussed.

393   Mor, V.; Sherwood, S.; Gutkin, C. (1986). A national study of residential care of the aged. The Gerontologist, 26(4), 405-417.
Residential care homes (domiciliary care, congregate care, or adult foster care homes) are seen as a possible alternative. A national survey using 1980 data, supplemented with a five-state sample, reveals wide variations among facilities serving more than 350,000 residents, more than half of whom are SSI recipients.

394   Morris, J.N.; Sherwood, S. (1984). Informal support resources for vulnerable elderly persons: Can they be counted on, why do they work? International Journal of Aging and Human Development. 18(2), 81-98.
Informal support system resiliency is analyzed for approximately 700 persons in varied settings. Data indicate that the support networks are pervasive and generally contain two or more informal helpers, and that the the mix of persons in the network vary considerably.

395   Morris, R. Alternatives to nursing home care: A proposal. (1971). Washington DC: US Senate. Special Committee on Aging. Committee Print, 26p.
Asserts that between 250,000 and 500,000 persons are institutionalized for reasons other than medical needs; proposes a personal care organization model. Part II by Levinson Policy Institute, Brandeis University, gives details of the model; Part III describes Federal role.

396   Musser, M.J.; Haber, P.A. (1973). Alternatives to hospitalization: The VA's experience. Perspective on Aging, 2(6). 8-11.
Almost 10 years after the Veterans Administration began a number of initiatives to improve hospital aftercare of significant numbers of veterans, two VA officials associated with their development give a positive progress report.

397   National Association of State Units on Aging. (1985). Primary caregivers: Support systems, A synthesis of issues and findings. US Department of Health and Human Services, Office of Human Development Services. 33p.
Focuses on the informal caregiving network and finds that OHDS demonstration projects may be categorized as: direct strengthening of informal caregivers or a caregiving network, linking informal caregivers with formal services agencies, and developing or sustaining mutual help groups.

398   National Association of Area Agencies on Aging. (1983). Community-based long term care statement. Washington DC: 18p.
A policy statement identifying the role of area agencies in developing comprehensive long term care service systems at client and community levels. Discusses existing Older Americans Act mandates and suggests new legislation providing greater specificity.

399   National Conference on Social Welfare. (1981). Long term care: In search of solutions. Washington DC: 32p.
A brief, incisive summary of present and future challenges to long term care, as compared to present deficiencies. A chapter on "Looking Ahead" foresees little if any increase in Federal support; new strategies include regulatory change, private sector roles, self help, and more use of paraprofessionals.

400   National Voluntary Organizations for Independent Living for the Aging. (1978). The 'at-risk' elderly: Community service approaches. Washington DC: The National Council on the Aging, 86p.
Reports on Operation Independence, a three-year Administration on Aging-funded project demonstrating ways to increase collaborative efforts among local voluntary, private, and public agencies to increase in-home and supportive services. Finds significant local resources can be mobilized.

401   Nelson, D. (1985) A community care program Perspective on Aging, 14(4), 12-14.
A summary of the Wisconsin Community Options Program, begun in 1982 with a $2 million state appropriation and expected to have a $42 million budget by 1988. Older Americans Act, Title XX, and Medicaid among funding sources. Empowering client decisions a key working principle.

402   Newcomer, R.; Friss, L. (1979). Housing in the continuum of care. Genera-
       tions, 3(3) 13-15.
Argues that housing and social services must be recognized as a central component
in the long term care system. Federal legislation and studies, however, are usually
"limited to expansion of categorical funding and better coordination of existing
services." Land use planners urged to heed a growing need.

403   Oriol, W.E. (1985). The complex cube of long term care: The case for next-
       step solutions—now. Washington DC: American Health Planning Association,
       337p.
Challenges "gaps that now separate long term care solutions" beginning in jurisdictional conflicts in the Congress and extending to the states and private and
voluntary sectors. Emphasizes positive gains in some states, communities and the
Veterans Administration. Informative appendices, including a glossary.

404   Rubenstein, L.Z.; Rhee, L.; Kane, R.L.. (1982). The role of geriatric assess-
       ment units in caring for the elderly: an analytic review. Journal of Geron-
       tology, 37, 513-521.
Encouraging results reported by special units designed to assess the spectrum of
geriatric needs, to effect a comprehensive care plan, and often to provide initial
steps toward rehabilitation. Specific projects in Canada and the United States summarized in table form. Cost-effectiveness usually demonstrated.

405   Sager, A. (1983). A proposal for promoting more adequate long term care for
       the elderly. The Gerontologist, 23(1), 13-17.
"Fears of uncontrollable costs have blocked approval of Federal legislation to
expand non-institutional long-term care benefits" at just the time, it is argued,
that a great deal is known about needs assessment, equitable service allocation,
and the effectiveness of in-home service. Mutual aid schemes proposed.

406   Scharlach, A.; Frenzel, C. (1986). An evaluation of institution-based respite
       care. The Gerontologist. 26(1), 77-81.
Findings from a survey of 99 caregivers using a Veterans Administration respite
service used to argue that policy makers should examine respite care more closely
as an important link in long term care continuums, since caregiver needs are now
largely unmet.

407   Schlesinger, M. (1986). On the limits of expanding health care reform:
       Chronic care in prepaid settings. The Milbank Memorial Quarterly, 64(2),
       189-215.
Explores Medicare reimbursement for beneficiaries enrolled in health maintenance
organizations and other forms of prepaid health care; urges policymakers to become more cognizant of the limitations of prepayment even as they adapt to new
forces in the health marketplace.

408   Sicker, M. (1978). Wanted: A national long term care policy. Perspective on
       Aging, 7(3), 26-27.
An Administration on Aging official notes legislative enactments giving that agency
specific responsibilities for developing long term care services, but warns against
inadequate funding and confusing mandates. Calls the Health Care Financing Administration the central focal point for long term care.

409 Skellie, F.A.; Coan, R.E. (1980). Community-based long-term care and mortality: Preliminary findings of Georgia's alternative health services project. The Gerontologist, 20(3), 372-379.
A Federal-State demonstration project using Medicaid as primary source of reimbursement provides adult day rehabilitation and home delivered services in a 17-county target area. Evaluation of 267 clients shows positive effect on mortality and potential Medicaid savings. Full implications await detailed cost figures.

410 Sommers, T. (1985). Long term care: Biggest dilemma, toughest problem, greatest challenge. Perspective on Aging, 14(4), 9-11,20.
The president of the Older Women's League asks for help in making long term care a women's issue, calling "caregiver" a euphemism for closest female relative. To make "a viable, humane long term care" system in the United States, she offers 10 suggestions, including mutual help support groups.

411 Steinhauer, M.B. (1982). Geriatric foster care: A prototype design and implementation issues. The Gerontologist, 22(3), 293-300.
An intensive policy analysis of geriatric foster care—the use of private family residences for care of nonrelated elderly—leads to suggested prototype allowing residents to remain in the community while obtaining needed supportive services. Policy changes suggested. Useful summary of services in 11 states.

412 Taber, M.A.; Anderson, S.; Rogers, C.J. (1980). Implementing community care in Illinois: Issues of cost and targeting in a statewide program. The Gerontologist, 20(3), 380-388.
All Illinois 60+ persons in danger of "premature or unnecessary institutionalization" became eligible for chore/housekeeping, homemaker, home health, and adult care services under a Community Care bill. After six months of operation, authors find cost effectiveness inconclusive, but regard program as notable.

413 Trager, B. (1976). Adult day facilities for treatment, health care and related services. Washington DC: US Senate Special Committee on Aging. SuDoc Y4.Ag4:T71, 116p.
Describes day care centers as providers of group care and services during the day in a safe, comfortable environment. Summarizes studies designed to test cost effectiveness, but reports that the fundamental difficulty is fragmented Federal funding and lack of clearcut policy.

414 US Congress. Office of Technology Assessment. (1985). Technologies, functional impairment, and long term care. In: Technology and aging in America. Washington DC: OTA-BA-264, 185-245.
Influence of Federal funding mechanisms in shaping long term care system is traced, concern about cost control appears to conflict with efforts to assure access to needed services. Potential use of technologies for assessment, assistive devices, rehabilitation techniques, and caregiver assistance.

415 US Congressional Budget Office. (1977). Long term care for the elderly and disabled. GPO 83-665 O-77-2, 62p.
Examines the extent of need for long term care, the degree to which demand is met by current public programs, and several alternative means of satisfying demand and organizing services. Note: A technical paper, Long Term Care: Actuarial Cost Estimates, accompanies.

416 US Department of Health and Human Services, Office of the Inspector General. (1982). Board and care homes. 82p.
A study of Federal and state actions intended to safeguard the health and safety of board and care residents, many of whom rely upon Federal income maintenance programs for payment of fees. Recommendations suggest ways in which Federal agencies can work cooperatively with states.

417 US House of Representatives. Select Committee on Aging. (1985). America's elderly at risk. Y4.Ag4/2:E12/38, 34p.
Finds a "frighteningly high financial risk" facing those elderly with chronic and disabling illnesses. Elderly health costs, rising markedly because of Medicare cost-sharing increases and other factors, said to be an out-of-pocket $1,660 in 1985 for health and long term care, and a probable $2,583 in 1990.

418 US Veterans Administration. (1984). Caring for the older veteran. 87p.
Describes a very rapidly aging veteran population as a major challenge to the VA, and suggests that VA solutions to health care problems "may become models for dealing with these same needs in the larger population." VA's efforts to establish integrated long term care systems discussed.

419 Von Behren, R. (1985). Adult day care: Progress, problems, and promise. Perspective on Aging, 14(6), 5,39.
Cites multiple Federal and other funding sources for adult day care as a major problem, but reports "remarkable progress" made since early 1970s. This introduction to a special edition about adult day care summarizes other issues including usefulness of private insurance and state initiatives.

420 Weiler, P.G. (1974). Cost-Effective analysis: A quandary for geriatric health care systems. The Gerontologist, 14(5), 414-417.
Argues that there cannot be rational cost-effective analysis of the geriatric health care system "as long as it remains imbedded in a system which is essentially only acute-care oriented." Suggests a strategy for a long term care approach, using as a model a geriatric day care center in Kentucky.

421 Weissert, W.G. (1985). Home and community based care: The cost-effectiveness trap. Generations, 9(4), 47-49.
Argues that many studies challenge assumptions that noninstitutional care is less costly than nursing homes, but warns that the cost-effectiveness argument is self-defeating and that other rationales are more effective. Urges broader program eligibilty to include all dependent people.

422 Williams, W.S.; Lidoff, L. (1985). State support for respite care: Report of an exploratory survey. Perspective on Aging, 9(2), 13-14.
Programs including Medicaid and the Older Americans Act are identified as funding sources for states that are providing relief to frail older persons. Sixteen states have enacted legislation; a number are tied to demonstration programs and Medicaid Section 2176 waivers; wide variations exist.

423 Winn, S.; McCaffree, K.M. (1979). Issues involved in the development of a prepaid capitation plan for long-term care services. The Gerontologist, 19(2), 184-190.

To replace fee-for-service as the basis for payment of long term care services under publicly funded programs, authors propose establishment of prepaid capitation service. Early, limited capitation demonstration projects discussed, as are alternative approaches to develop such plans.

424   Wylie, M.; Austin, Carol. (1978) Policy foundations for case management: Consequences for the frail elderly. Journal of Gerontological Social Work. 1(1). 7-18.
Concerns about a model for coordinated services for the elderly are discussed; analysis of other policy matters includes considerations that "elevate the needs of the elderly to a higher position than survival requirements of provider agencies."

MEDICAID

425   Harrington, C.; Estes, C.L.; Lee, P.R.; Newcomer, R.J. (1986). Effects of state Medicaid policies on the aged. The Gerontologist, 26(4). 437-443.
Compares trends from 1978-1982 in eight sample states and their relationship to national averages. Cost containment pressures found to have widely varying effects; an anticipated substantial curtailment of eligibility did not occur, but other constraints reduced service growth.

426   Intergovernmental Health Policy Project. (1985). Major changes in state Medicaid and indigent care programs. Washington DC: George Washington University, 16p.
Continues annual reviews of state actions to adjust Medicaid to meet new goals and cut costs. Finds that at least 13 states expanded some services even while others were constricting eligibility or making other cuts.

427   Joe, T.; Meltzer, J.; Farrow, F. (1983). Restructuring Medicaid: An agenda for change—summary report of the National Study Group on State Medicaid Policies. Washington DC: Center for the Study of Social Policy. 58p.
Criticizes Medicaid for encompassing multiple and often disparate objectives and services. Proposes a Federally-financed and administered national primary health care system for low-income individuals. A state-administered continuing care system would provide "a full range of health and social long term care services...".

428   Oriol, W.E. (1985). Medicaid essential—provides critical protection for 23 million. Perspective on Aging, 14(4), 4-8.
Provides a 20th anniversary perspective on Medicaid accomplishments and shortcomings. Concerns about rising expenditures described; examples of proposed restructuring offered. Study guide, extensive references.

429   US House of Representatives. Select Committee on Aging. (1982). Medicaid fraud: A case history in the failure of state enforcement. SuDoc Y4.Ag4/2: M46/13, 103p.
Complains about "shortsighted Federal and state regulations" accused of hampering work of State Medicaid fraud units established at that time in 30 states. Offers recommendations for reform.

430   US Senate. Special Committee on Aging, Subcommittee on Long Term Care. (1976). Fraud and abuse among practitioners participating in the Medicaid program. SuDoc Y4.Ag4:M46/6, 287p.

Offers findings from undercover and other investigations of "Medicaid mills," or small clinics providing questionable or illegal services in low-income areas. Medicaid regulatory gaps discussed; recommendations made.

MEDICARE

431 Ball, R.E. (1978). Health care for the elderly. In: Ball, R.E. Social Security today and tomorrow. New York: Columbia University Press, 96-105.
Emphasizes threats of health care costs to Medicare recipients even while citing accomplishments of that program. Suggests steps to bring functionally dependent elders under a comprehensive long term care program including home-based services, as well as institutional care.

432 Bayer, R. (1985). Coping with cost containment. In: Moody, H.R. (Ed.). Ethics and Aging. Generations, 9(2), 39-42.
Views Medicare's prospective payment system as potential threat to quality of and access to care and offers models to assure treatment even in "marginal" cases. Describes increases in Medicare participants' "cost-sharing" as a means of "reprivatizing" the cost of the program.

433 Bayer, R. (1984). Will the first Medicare generation be the last? The Hastings Center Report, 14(3), p.17.
Summarizes Medicare financial difficulties and arguments to make it a need-based program. Warns: "This is the first generation of elderly Americans to be freed from the fear of the potential financial devastation brought on by illness. Changes in Medicare now being considered could well make it the last."

434 Berk, M.L.; Wilensky, G.R. (1985). Health care of the poor elderly: Supplementing Medicare. The Gerontologist, 25(3), 311-314.
Develops estimates showing that out-of-pocket health care costs increased markedly in 1977-82 among poor and near-poor elderly, particularly among those ineligible for Medicaid. Purchasers of supplemental insurance found to have heaviest personal costs. Suggests selective exemptions.

435 Birnbaum, H.G.; Kidder, D. (1984). What does hospice cost? American Journal of Public Health, 74(7), 689-697.
Presents the preliminary results of the 1981-1983 National Hospice Study, finding that hospice care can cost less than conventional care under varying circumstances. Note: See related editorial, in same issue (p.7-8) by Bruce Vladeck, The Limits of Cost-Effectiveness.

436 Brody, S.J.; Magel, J.S. (1984). DRGs—The second revolution in health care for the elderly. Journal of the American Geriatrics Society, 32(9), 676-679.
Diagnosis related groups (DRGs)—the basis of a Medicare Prospective Payment System adopted in 1983—said to provide hospitals with incentives to develop "short term long-term-care" services and facilities. Foresees a "major allocation of acute care medical funds to long-term care."

437 Brown, E.R. (1984). Medicare and Medicaid: Band-aids for the older and poor. In: Sidel, V.W.; Sidel, R. (Eds.). Reforming medicine: Lessons of the last quarter century. New York: Pantheon Books, 50-76.
Acknowledges achievements of the two programs, but criticizes "the separation of

medical care for the poor from the program for the elderly," "regressive" financing, and integration of both programs into the existing market system. Calls for a
national health service.

**438   Campion, F.D. (1984). The expansion of access: Medicare and Medicaid. In:
Campion, F.D. The AMA and US health policy since 1940. Chicago Review
Press, 253-283.**
This chapter in an authorized history of the American Medical Association acknowledges that governmental insurance was needed for many older Americans who
could not obtain private protection in the early 1960s. It also gives AMA reasons
for nevertheless opposing Medicare.

**439   Davis, K.; Rowland, D. (1986). Medicare policy: New directions for health and
long term care. Baltimore: Johns Hopkins University Press, 137p.**
Critically reviews reasons for current bifurcation of acute and long term care
coverage. Authors' proposal for an integrated system includes a merger of Medicare's hospital and medical parts with an income related premium, elective long
term care insurance, and other system reforms. Useful appendix.

**440   Feder, J.M. (1977). Medicare: The politics of Federal hospital insurance. Lex-
ington MA: Lexington books, 177p.**
A valuable account of factors leading to Medicare implementation policies that, in
the view of the author, led to reimbursement practices giving wide leeway and advantages to hospitals and other medical providers.

**441   Fuchs, V.R. (1984). "Though much is taken": Reflections on aging, health, and
medical care. Milbank Memorial Fund Quarterly, 62(2), 143-166.**
Puts Medicare financing issue into a broad context of economic and social trends,
including unresolved retirement and employment issues and health system structure
deficiencies. Asks for special attention to economic issues arising from high costs
of care for the dying.

**442   Greer, D.S.; Mor, V. (1985). How Medicare is altering the hospice movement.
The Hastings Center Report, 15(5), 5-9.**
Traces varying hospice response since Congress enacted 1982 legislation authorizing
Medicare reimbursement for certified programs. Complains about sparse attention
given to the National Hospice Study and emerging policy dilemmas and conflicts.

**443   Harvard Medicare Project (1986). Medicare: Coming of age—a proposal for
reform. Cambridge MA: Center for Health Policy and Management. 95p.**
A diverse group of physicians, gerontologists, social scientists, economists, lawyers,
and others call for comprehensive Medicare reform, with government continuing to
play a central role. A major proposal calls for Medicare Parts A (hospital) and B
(medical) to be combined into a single, mandatory program.

**444   Howard, E.F. (1985). Medicare cornerstone of health protection. Perspective
on Aging, 14(3), 4-6.**
Medicare, on 20th anniversary of enactment, regarded as legislative recognition
"that the Federal Government has a legitimate role, even a central one, in meeting society's obligation to assure equitable access to health care for its citizens."
Shortcomings recognized, but program called essential.

445   Iglehart, J.K. (1985). Medicare turns to HMOs. New England Journal of Medicine, 312(2), 132-136.
An informative account of Federal interest and experiments leading to 1982 legislation authorizing greater efforts to enroll Medicare beneficiaries in health maintenance organizations. Examines problems arising in demonstration projects and foresees considerable impact upon health care system.

446   Iverson, L.H.; Polich, C.L. (1985). The future of Medicare and HMOs. Excelsior MN: Interstudy Center for Aging and Long Term Care, 39p.
An optimistic view of the potential role of health maintenance organizations in serving Medicare clients. Gives excellent account of 1982 legislation intended to encourage HMO Medicare enrollments, and survey findings.

447   Long, S.H.; Settle, R.F. (1984). Medicare and the disabled elderly: Origins and outcomes. Milbank Memorial Fund Quarterly. 62(4), 609-656.
An authoritative account of Medicare's progress in broadening access to health care even for low-income persons, reducing discriminatory practices against minorities, and making care more available in rural areas. Despite substantial improvement, deficiencies recognized and described.

448   Marmor, T.F. (1980). The politics of Medicare. New York: Aldine Press, 150p.
An informative account of the legislative struggles and principal antagonists involved in the final maneuvers for enactment of Medicare in 1965. Useful glossary.

449   Melemed, B.B. (1983). Formulating a public policy for long term care: A different view. Perspective on Aging, 12(3), 4-5, 30.
Challenges view (see entry 454) that Medicare should be the primary vehicle long term care reform. Doubts "that... centralizing long term care decisionmaking authority under the control of a physician--and by extension, the medical establishment--will achieve the intended goals." Gives four principles for reform.

450   Merritt, R.E.; Potemken, D.B. (Eds.) (1982). Medigap: Issues and update. Washington DC: Intergovernmental Health Policy Project, George Washington University. 101p.
Heavy outlays by Medicare participants for private insurance to cover program gaps are accompanied by consumer confusion over the actual protection provided. Summarizes the myriad state actions and Federal attempts to act circumspectly in an arena traditionally regulated at the state level.

451   Palmore, E.B. (1986). Trends in the health of the aged. The Gerontologist, 26(3), 298-302.
Cites data showing consistent, substantial relative health gains for elderly from 1961-81. Medicare and Medicaid called contributing factors. Service delivery professionals told they "need not fear that the increasing numbers of elders will be compounded by increased illness and disability among the average elderly person."

452   Schrimper, R.A.; Clark, R.L. (1985). Health expenditures and elderly adults. Journal of Gerontology, 40(2), 235-243.
Household expenditure data for five groups of elderly indicate that increases in direct health expenditures of the elderly are likely to lead to significant reductions in food, housing, and transportation expenditures, even with Medicare, because of Medicare cost-sharing and sharply rising health costs.

453   Schweiker, R.S. (1982). Report to Congress: Hospital prospective payment for
       Medicare. US Department of Health and Human Services, 132p.
As mandated by statute, the HHS Secretary presents the case for implementing a
new reimbursement system that "will establish Medicare as a prudent buyer of
hospital services." Evidence is presented identifying costly aspects of existing
cost-based retrospective system.

454   Somers, A.R. (1983). Medicare and long-term care. Perspective on Aging,
       12(2), 5-8, 28.
Updates arguments for her proposal, first made in 1981, to make Medicare more
responsive to long term care needs through elimination of prohibition against cus-
todial care, use of prospective payment for all Medicare services, and establishment of "reasonable, non-deterrent" patient cost-sharing formulas.

455   Starr, P. (1983). Redistribution without reorganization. In: Starr, P. The
       social transformation of American medicine. New York: Basic Books, 363-
       378.
Uses Medicare as one of several examples of the "politics of accommodation" during the "Liberal Years" of health legislation, asserting that doctors and hospitals
withheld cooperation from a government program to secure long run advantages.

456   US General Accounting Office. (1976). History of the rising costs of the Med-
       icare and Medicaid and attempts to control these costs: 1966-75. GAO
       MWD-76-93, 126p.
Finds that health cost inflation was the major factor in a $10.4 billion rise in
Medicare costs, and that greater participation and increased use of hospitals
played relatively minor roles. Inflation was also a major factor in rising Medicaid
costs. Prior GAO recommendations discussed; additional proposals offered.

457   US House of Representatives. Committee on Ways and Means. (1983). Confer-
       ence on the future of Medicare. Subcommittee on Health. SuDoc Y4.W36:
       WMCP98-20, 152p.
Offers papers commissioned for an unusual exploratory conference by the Ways and
Means Committee, the Congressional Budget Office, and the Congressional Research Service. Useful historical background; financing issues dominant; feasibility
of Medicare voucher system discussed.

458   US Senate. Committee on Finance. (1970). Medicare and Medicaid: Problems,
       issues, and alternatives. SuDoc Y4.F49:M46/6, 277p.
Declares that Medicare and Medicaid "are in serious financial trouble," with far-
reaching consquences for health care costs and individual citizens. Offers numerous
recommendations on reimbursement and other matters.

459   US Senate. Special Committee on Aging. (1984). Medicare and the health
       costs of older Americans: The extent and effects of cost sharing. SuDoc
       Y4.Ag4:Sprt.98-166, 38p.
Evaluates proposals for proposed increases in costs paid by Medicare beneficiaries
in the light of the level of protection afforded by the program. Finds that future
cost sharing is not likely to have significant impact on Medicare expenditures, but
would fall hard upon the sickest and low-income.

460   US Senate. Special Committee on Aging. Subcommittee on Health of the Elderly. (1964). Blue Cross and private health insurance coverage of older Americans. Committee Print, 153p.
At a critical juncture in the legislative struggle for Medicare, this report presented evidence that "private health insurance is unable to provide the large majority of our 18 million older Americans with adequate hospital protection at reasonable premium cost."

MENTAL HEALTH

461   Aronson, M.K.; Katzman, R. (1982). Making the system more responsive. Generations, 7(1), 47–49.
Alzheimer's Disease and other dementias viewed as a burgeoning challenge, requiring education of the general public and health professionals, family support services, policy changes making a continuum of community services more available, and "creative financing" of health care programs.

462   Butler, R.N. (1984). How Alzheimer's became a public issue. Generations, 9(1), 33–35.
A first-hand account of actions by the National Institute on Aging to marshall research findings and public knowledge so that health/science policy would be directed to the severe social and personal damage done by an insidious disease.

463   Butler, R.N. (1970). Immediate and long-range dangers to transfer of elderly patients from state hospitals to community facilities. The Gerontologist, 10(4), 259–260.
Calls wholesale transfer of elderly psychiatric patients from mental hospital to various care facilities "a tragic abdication of the responsibility of medicine in general and psychiatry in particular." Describes many nursing homes as unable to care for such patients.

464   Butler, R.N.; Lewis, M.I. (1977). How to keep people at home: In: Aging and mental health: Positive psychosocial approaches. (Second edition.) Saint Louis: C.V. Mosby Company, 211–235.
Essentially a summary of considerations arising when efforts are made to avoid institutionalization, this informative chapter also gives brief summaries of the advantages and limitations of public programs receiving Federal assistance for the ostensible purpose of making community care more available.

465   Donahue, W.T. (1978). What about our responsibility toward the abandoned elderly? The Gerontologist, 18(2), 102–111.
Deinstitutionalization, or discharge of patients or residents from state mental hospitals, is portrayed as a shocking policy failure, caused by faulty planning and other factors. Older persons were among those caught in the exodus, but details about their fates are sparse. Housing seen as key need.

466   Donahue, W.; Oriol, W.E. (Eds.). (1983). Housing the elderly deinstitutionalized mental patient. Psychiatric Quarterly (Special Issue), 55(2/3), 224p.
Informative papers by eminent authors explore the needs and problems of older persons in need of rehabilitation after being released from mental hospitals "into the community", often without access to care and services, or merely "reinstitutionalized" into nursing homes.

467   Federal Council on the Aging. (1978). Mental health and the aging: Recommendations for action. DHEW Publication OHDS 80-20960, 126p.
Includes text of the Secretary's Committee on the Mental Health and Illness of the Elderly and report of the Task Panel on the Elderly of the President's Commission on Mental Health. The May 1978 Secretary's Committee report makes recommendations on future care, research and training needs and care of elders in institutions. Task Panel, in February 1978, offers policy options.

468   Goldman, E.B.; Woog, P. (1975). Mental health in nursing homes training project: 1972-1973. The Gerontologist, 15(2), 119-128.
A partial response to the needs of rapidly rising numbers of mentally impaired elders in nursing homes is provided by this National Institute of Mental Health-funded project. Schools of Nursing and Social Work of Adelphi University in Garden City NY cooperated to develop greater staff knowledge and sensitivity.

469   Grady, S.; James, M. (1983). Michigan group tackles big problem. Perspective on Aging, 12(1), 14-15,24.
Aging and mental health agencies work together to design and provide services to older adults with mental problems. A state report, Are they worth it?, provides guiding principles and objectives. Federal funds from the National Institute of Mental Health, Older Americans Act used in program evolution.

470   Gurian, B.S. (1978). Mental health and the aging. In: Brookbank, J.W. (Ed.). Improving the quality of health care for the elderly. Gainesville FL: University of Florida Center for Gerontological Studies and Programs. 68-78.
Mental health care of the elderly said to have "a long, sordid history of neglect." Community mental health centers established in the 1960s put low priority on aging; only a dozen have comprehensive services for the elderly. Continuity of care is needed, but "treatment programs too often follow the available funding."

471   Hagebak, J.E.; Hagebak, B.R. (1983). Meeting the mental health needs of the elderly: Issues and action steps. Aging, Nos.335-336, 26-31.
An informative review of Federal policy through enactment of the 1980 Mental Health Systems Act—which identified the elderly as an underserved population in need of priority attention—and a mental health block grant that succeeded it in 1981. Suggests ways for governmental units to collaborate.

472   Heckler, M.M. (1985). Alzheimer's disease—a top priority. Human Development News, August 1985, p.1,8.
The Secretary of Health and Human Services gives reasons for establishing a Departmental Task Force on Alzheimer's Disease in 1983 and its relationship to family support issues. Role of Older American Act network discussed.

473   Kahn, R.L. (1975). The mental health system and the future aged. The Gerontologist, 15(1), Pt. II, 24-31.
Treatment of elderly under varying "ideologies"—including deinstitutionalization—is examined; author argues that the mental health revolution of the 1960s and 1970s has "led to their [the elderly] dropping out of the psychiatric system." Recommends a decentralized, de-medicalized system with care continuity.

474 Liptzin, B. (1984). Canadian and US systems of care for the mentally ill
     elderly. The Gerontologist, 24(2), 174-178.
Equal access to all mental health services is not assured by Canada's universal
health system; elderly patients may be underserved there, as in the United States,
but with significant variations. Acute psychiatric services are more readily accessible in Canada; Canadian nursing homes have special care programs.

475 Michigan Department of Mental Health. (1980). Are they worth it? A report
     of the Mental Health and Aging Advisory Group, 57p.
A landmark report, during a time of economic upheaval in Michigan, urging joint
state/Federal action to serve older adults. Reviews the care spectrum from state
hospitals to nursing homes. Adds: "We acknowledge limited resources as a reality,
not as an excuse."

476 Nardone, M. (1980). Characteristics predicting community care for mentally
     impaired older persons. The Gerontologist, 20(6), 661-668.
Pennsylvania counties were examined in a study of relationships between community and institutional care for the mentally impaired elderly. Nursing home bed
availability was a strong predictor of institutionalization. Author recommends "a
focused community service strategy, based on research."

477 Oriol, W.E. (1980). Housing the elderly deinstitutionalized mental hospital
     patient in the community. Washington DC: International Center for Social
     Gerontology, 167p.
Federal programs analyzed to show limited usefulness to elderly persons released
from mental hospitals without suitable community services to assist them, the
greatest gap being in suitable living quarters. Examples of positive programs given;
a provisional policy agenda offered. Extensive bibliography.

478 Santore, A.F.; Diamond, H. (1974). The role of a community mental health
     center in developing services to the aging: The older adult project. The Ger-
     ontologist, 14(3), 201-206.
Unresponsiveness to the elderly in community mental health centers is challenged
at a West Philadelphia CMHC. Describes bureaucratic and attitudinal barriers to
care for 65+ persons and center's collaboration with local clergy to overcome
problems. Older case aides recruited for outreach, other services.

479 Spence, D.L.; Cohen, S.; Kowalski, C. (1975). Mental health, age, and com-
     munity living. The Gerontologist, 15(1), 77-82.
A Rhode Island project provides 14-week programs for mental hospital clients aged
50 to 80 outside the hospital grounds to prepare for placement in the community.
Multi-agency cooperation described in training and in helping clients adjust to the
community. A key problem is housing options shortage.

480 US General Accounting Office. (1982). The elderly remain in need of mental
     health services. GAO/HRD-82-112. 26p.
A survey made just before implementation of a mental health block grant confirms
earlier criticisms that legislative mandates for improved services to elderly at community mental health centers had not been translated into effective action. Mental
health problems in nursing homes called "unrecognized and untreated."

481   US Senate. Special Committee on Aging. (1971). <u>Mental health care and the</u>
      <u>elderly: Shortcomings in public policy.</u> S.Report 92-423, 194p.
Cites testimony and studies indicating significant deterioration in mental health
services for older persons in the 1960s. Medicare and Medicaid shortcomings
described, as are unfortunate aspects of deinstitutionalization. Six project studies
give examples of effective treatment or support.

NURSING HOMES

482   Anderson, N.N.; Stone, L.B. (1969). Nursing homes: Research and public policy.
      <u>The Gerontologist, 9,</u> 214-218.
Acknowledges nursing home problems, but urges identification of "suitable action
points for remedying the situation." Suggests attention be given to matching of
services to patients, quality control systems, and use of market mechanisms (including new reimbursement methods to reward efficient care delivery).

483   Baldwin, C.Y.; Bishop, C.E. (1984). Return to nursing home investment:
      Issues for public policy. <u>Health Care Financing Review,</u> 5(4), 43-52.
Develops a theoretical framework for analyzing return under typical state reimbursement systems, which attempt to meet multiple public policy goals including
access, quality, and cost containment. Offers possible new approachs to capital
compensation.

484   Brody, E.M. (1973). A million Procrustean beds. <u>The Gerontologist,</u> 13(4),
      430-435.
Traces public policy contradictions that tend to produce uniformity by severe
methods in nursing homes, and offers an alternative under which such a facility
would "evolve as a new model with its own identity, rather than as a patchwork
of borrowed patterns."

485   Butler, R.N. (1971). The public interest: Report No.1. <u>Aging and Human De-</u>
      <u>velopment,</u> 2(1), 139-141.
Proposes that the $2 billion "that the Federal Government contributes to proprie-
tary nursing homes be diverted to the creation of nonprofit social utilities,"
excluding the "expensive middle-man insurance industry." A National Personal Care
Corps recommended to supplement professional staff.

486   Dunlop, B.D. (1979). <u>The growth of nursing home care.</u> Lexington MA: Lex-
      ington Books, 171p.
Chronic excess demand for nursing home care found common by end of 1964-74
study period. Comprehensive planning mechanisms deemed essential to guide future
growth and to link with much-needed services and supportive residences. Excellent
appendices include Federal actions chronology, 1950-1974.

487   Follingstad, M.; Frank, B. (1978). <u>The plight of the nurses aide in America's</u>
      <u>nursing homes: An obstacle to quality care for nursing home residents.</u>
      Washington DC: National Citizens Coalition for Nursing Home Reform, 41p.
Finds that 70 percent of nursing home residents' human interactions are with nurses aides. Recommends preservice training and certification of aides as a Medicare
and Medicaid requirement.

488 Fottler, M.D.; Smith, H.L.; James, W.L. (1981). Profits and patient care quality in nursing homes: Are they compatible? The Gerontologist, 21(5), 532-538.

A study of 43 proprietary nursing homes in California focuses on four measures of
quality for patient care and finds a consistent negative relationship between
profitability and patient care quality. A fundamental difficulty is that public policy
has not clearly defined the desired level for such quality.

489 Frank, B.; Holder, E.L. (1983). Consumer statement of principles for the
nursing home regulatory system: State licensure and Federal certification
programs. Washington DC: National Citizens' Coalition for Nursing Home
Reform. 131p.
Explores fundamental enforcement issues at a critical time in the development of
Federal standards, stressing need for adequate budgeting. NCCNHR was joined by
37 other national organizations in presenting this document. Excellent overview;
useful source material.

490 Gold, J.G.; Kaufman, S.M. (1970). Development of care of the elderly: Tracing the history of institutional facilities. The Gerontologist, 10(4), 262-274.
Though making only tangential mention of public programs in the United States,
this is an invaluable reference for researchers seeking historical perspective (dating back to Biblical times) on values and practices related to institutional care.
Close attention given to the rise of homes for the aged.

491 Holder, E.L. (1985). Nursing home quality care sought. Perspective on Aging,
14(5), 19,29.
Summarizes potentially positive developments related to Federal role in assuring
quality nursing home care. Court decisions, Institute of Medicine study of regulatory issues cited. A detailed description a new Health Care Financing Administration Patient Care and Services (PaCS) review system is given.

492 Institute of Medicine (Committee on Nursing Home Regulation). (1986).
Improving the quality of care in nursing homes. Washington DC: National
Academy Press, 430p.
A definitive response to rising Congressional and public concern about shortcomings
in longstanding regulatory policy, offering far-ranging recommendations related to
quality standards, consumer advocacy, bed supply, and survey techniques. Cost factors discussed.

493 Johnson, C.L; Grant, L.A. (1985). Nursing homes in American society. Baltimore: Johns Hopkins University Press, 220p.
Part III has useful chapters on policy issues and an admirable summary in table
form of assistance from Federal programs. Legal and regulatory constraints are
discussed. A good introduction to the subject; numerous references.

494 Kane, R.L.; Bell, R.; Riegler, S.; Wilson, A.; Kane, R.A.. (1983). Assessing
the outcomes of nursing home patients. Journal of Gerontology, 38(4), 385-
393.
Multi-dimensional measures of nursing home patients' functions are used in four
skilled Los Angeles nursing homes with a reputation for good care. Authors find it
is possible to obtain valid data from nursing home residents on outcomes of treatment. Suggests steps to improve reimbursement standards.

495   Kastenbaum, R.; Candy, S.E. (1973). The 4% Fallacy: A methodological and empirical critique of extended care facility population statistics. The International Journal of Aging and Human Development, 4(1), 15-21.
Challenges the frequently cited cross-sectional finding that four percent of the 65-plus population are in nursing homes. Using practical measures, authors see a 20 percent likelihood of a 65+ person's dying in an institution. Asks for more sensitive Federal policy to improve quality of terminal care.

496   Kosberg, J.I. (1974). Making institutions accountable: Research and policy issues. The Gerontologist, 14(6), 510-516.
Finds that lack of guidance and control from public policy has intensified accountability problems of nursing homes. Another problem is lack of knowledge about quality of care standards. Urges an outcome orientation for standards based upon both positive and negative sanctions.

497   Latt, B. (1970). Licensure of nursing home administrators—opportunity and challenge. The Gerontologist, 10(3), p.179.
An informative account of the early impact of a Federal law requiring States to establish programs for licensing nursing home administrators by July 1970. Useful for researchers of nursing home regulation; provides details on problems and ground-breaking efforts to comply with the law.

498   Manton, K.G.; Liu, K.; Cornelius, E.S. (1985). An analysis of the heterogeneity of US nursing home patients. Journal of Gerontology, 40(1), 34-36.
Review of individual and service chracteristics of two types of patients represented in the 1977 Nursing Home Survey identifies patient differences, providing "the advantage of defining a relatively small number of reimbursement options yet allowing for the true heterogeneity of individual patients."

499   Mendelson, M.A.; Hapgood, D. (1974). The political economy of nursing homes. In: Eisele, F.R. (Ed.). The political consequences of aging. The Annals of the American Academy of Political and Social Science. 415(September), 95-104.
Finds petty and large-scale fiscal abuses in nursing homes, which receive three-quarters of their income from government. Asserts that regulations are bypassed because of lack of public, governmental determination. Industry lobbyists described as influential at the state level, where Medicaid rates are set.

500   Mitchell, J.B. (1982). Physician visits to nursing homes. The Gerontologist, 22(1), 45-48.
Analysis of a 1977 physician survey indicates that only 47 percent of sample's general practitioners, internists, and cardiologists had made nursing home visits, despite Medicare and Medicaid requirements. Higher reimbursement levels may help, but other steps—including improved medical school training—discussed.

501   Monk, A.; Kaye, L.W. (1982). The ombudsman volunteer in the nursing home: Differential role perceptions of the patient representatives for the institutionalized aged. The Gerontologist, 22(2), 194-199.
A study of a New York City, Older American Act-funded program concludes that volunteer ombudsman—in resolving nursing home complaints—assume a broad range of practice behaviors. Legislative initiatives to foster a range of redress mechanisms are discussed; funding levels called inadequate.

502   Nixon, R.M. (1971). Steps to improve nursing homes. Aging, No.203, 3, 22-23.
Text of a speech given by President Nixon outlining an 8-point national program emphasizing enforcement efforts and short-term training for physicians,
nurses, social workers and other service providers. Goal is described as "improvement of existing substandard homes rather than their abolition."

503   Noam, E. (1975). Homes for the aged: Supervision and standards, a report on
the legal situation in European countries. US Department of Health, Education, and Welfare Publication (OHD) 75-20104, 93p.
Frequent references made to United States regulation of nursing homes in this
analysis of institutional assistance (in service flats, old people's homes, and geriatric nursing homes) in western and European nations. Includes chapter on reasons
for state control of homes.

504   Riportella-Muller, R.; Slesinger, D.P. (1982). The relationship of ownership
and size to quality and care in Wisconsin nursing homes. The Gerontologist,
22(4), 429-434.
Analysis of code violation and complaint data indicate fewer violations and complaints in nonprofit, smaller homes; large nonprofit homes tend to have more violations than large profit homes. Decommercialization of the industry will not
ensure correction; effective regulation, funding of alternative services needed.

505   Ruchlin, H.S. (1981). A new strategy for regulating long term care facilities.
In: Hudson, R.B. (Ed.). The aging in politics: Process and policy. Springfield
IL: Charles C. Thomas, 236-258.
Views incentive structure as essential for regulatory mechanisms capable of
effecting greater efficiency and higher quality. Serious efforts at reform are hin-
dered by lack of clearcut public policy on aging. Specific recommendations provided. Meaty references.

506   Smith, D.B. (1981). Long term care in transition: The regulation of nursing
homes. Washington DC: AUPHA Press, 170p.
New York State's experiences in attempting to improve institutional care said to
result in an intensified adversarial climate and a "coercive regulatory environment." Suggests regulatory reforms emphasizing decentralization and reapportion-
ment of resources and responsibilities.

507   Smith,   K.F.;   Bengston,   V.L.   (1979).   Positive   consequences   of
institutionalization: Solidarity between elderly parents and their middle-aged
children. The Gerontologist, 19(5). 438-447.
Open-ended interviews over two years with institutionalized residents and adult
child most involved with their care (N=100) lead to conclusion that several forms
of strengthened family ties occurred. Policymakers urged to consider such positive
family consequences to help institutional care reach its full potential.

508   US General Accounting Office. (1986). Medicaid: Methods for setting nursing
home rates should be improved. Washington DC: GAO/HRD 86-26 47p.
Congress, through enactment of the Omnibus Reconciliation Act of 1980, gave
states more flexibility in their nursing home reimbursement systems. This study
reviews prospective payment systems in seven states. It identifies "weaknesses in
each phase of the rate-setting process" and requests more Federal data collection.

509 US General Accounting Office. (1986). VA health care: Issues and concerns for VA nursing home programs. GAO/HRD-86-111BR, 41p.
Analyzes issues arising from the Veterans Administration proposal to redistribute its nursing home beds to 30 percent VA-owned, 40 percent community and 30 percent state, instead of 40, 40, and 20 percent respectively. In so doing, it provides a useful summary of the VA's nursing home programs.

510 US General Accounting Office. (1983). Medicaid and nursing home care: Cost increases and the need for services are creating problems for the states and the elderly. GAO/IPE-84-1, 172p.
Contrasts growing need for services among increasingly dependent residents and state efforts to contain costs. Evaluates tendency of Medicare Prospective Payment System to increase demand. Identifies utilization data gaps. Excellent appendix material.

511 US Senate. Special Committee on Aging. (1986). Nursing home care: The unfinished agenda. SuDoc Y1/4.Ag4:Sprt.99-160, 40p.
A two-year study shows that almost one-third of the Nation's 8,852 skilled nursing facilities fail to meet at least one basic standard assuring health and safety of residents. Staff recommendations made. State findings summarized. Case studies of chronic offenders in Washington DC, Georgia, California.

512 US Senate. Special Committee on Aging. Subcommittee on Long Term Care. (1975). What can be done in nursing homes: Positive aspects in long term care. SuDoc Y4.Ag.4:N93/5/No.6, 130p.
As one of a series on nursing home policy (see entry 513), this supporting paper describes innovative therapy and rehabilitation and personnel practices that maintain high standards despite difficulties caused by public program shortcomings. Value of public ombudsman programs discussed.

513 US Senate. Special Committee on Aging. Subcommittee on Long Term Care. (1974). Nursing home care in the United States: Failure in public policy. SuDoc Y4.Ag.4:N93/3/No.1, 161p.
Finds that "a coherent, constructive, and progressive national policy has not yet been developed to meet the long term care needs of the elderly." Examines Medicare and Medicaid shortcomings, failure to develop noninstitutional care, and regulatory gaps. Summarizes subsequent supporting papers on nine specific issues.

514 Vladeck, B.C. (1980). Unloving care: The nursing home tragedy. New York: Basic Books, 305p.
Declares that nursing home problems are really "a byproduct of broader social welfare policy but in a tangential fashion." Criticizes policymakers for failing to expand services outside the institution and for slighting health maintenance policies. A spirited, authoritative account.

515 Wershow, H.J. (1976). The four percent fallacy: Some further evidence and policy implications. The Gerontologist, 16(1), 52-55.
Forty-four percent of nursing home patient deaths occurred within 30 days of admission in this Alabama study of 460 such deaths. This factor alone gives credence to other studies indicating that the percentage of elderly in nursing homes at any given time is 4 percent.

516   Wilson, S.H. (1978). Nursing home patients' rights: Are they enforceable? The
      Gerontologist, 18(3), 255-261.
Medicare and Medicaid regulations provide a nursing home patient's bill of rights,
but article raises questions about persistence of deprivation of personal rights and
liberties. A proposal for a citation system of monetary penalties is advanced.
Obstacles to litigation in such cases described.

REHABILITATION

517   Brummel-Smith, K. (1984). Training health professionals. Generations, 8(4),
      47-50.
The co-director of a Federally-assisted rehabilitation center for the elderly at
Rancho Los Amigos, California, argues that all geriatrics should be seen as reha-
bilitative, and that publicly-supported and private medical training should foster a
positive orientation towards the disabled older person.

518   Brody, S.J. (1986). Impact of the formal support system on the rehabilitation
      of the elderly. In: Brody, S.J.; Ruff, G.E. (Eds.) Aging and rehabilitation:
      Advances in the state of the art. New York: Springer Publishing Co., 62-86.
An invaluable guide and critique of the separate Federal programs that address
varying eligibility groups and goals, but nevertheless can contribute to "comprehensive rehabilitation embedded in adequate psychosocial supports."

519   Brody, S.J.; Ruff, G.E. (Eds.). (1986). Aging and rehabilitation: Advances in
      the state of the art. New York: Springer Publishing Co., 378p.
Definitive papers from a conference organized by the Federally-assisted Rehabilitation Research and Training Center in Aging at the University of Pennsylvania. A
key theme: the need for "appropriate rehabilitation goals for this new target population, the disabled elderly.

520   Cromar, E. (1984). Research and the disabled elderly. Generations, 8(4),
      55-58.
Attributes much knowledge gain to research "that shatters the myth that 'disability' is inevitable and a normal consequence of aging." Gives research goals of the
National Institute of Handicapped Research and its two centers specializing in rehabilitation and the elderly. Other Federal agencies discussed.

521   Kaplan, J.; Ford, C.S. (1975). Rehabilitation for the elderly: An 11-year
      assessment. The Gerontologist, 15(5), 393-397.
High rate (61 percent) of discharge to independent living is made possible by team
rehabilitation effort including adequate social service staff. Federal retreat in
support for such services cited, despite evidence that "this type of health team
approach and the numbers of needed nursing home beds may be intertwined."

HOUSING

522   Abrams, P. (1983). Decent, affordable housing HUD's aim for older persons.
      Perspective on Aging, 12(3), 19,27.
An appraisal by the assistant secretary for housing, US Department of Housing and
Urban Development, of Administration's programs for low-income elderly. Estimates
that 15 percent of the older population cannot afford adequate shelter. Cites reasons for opposing a HUD office of elderly housing.

523   Bryant, D.S.; Turner, L.A. (1983). Cooperative housing is a self-help option
      for the elderly. Perspective on Aging, 12(2). 12-14.
Describes varying kinds of cooperative housing arising in the United States from "a
rich history of intentional, cooperative communities based on religious, ethnic,
political and economic ties." Federal programs that could be helpful listed, along
with difficulties in tapping them.

524   Carp, F.M. (1975). Long-range satisfaction with housing. The Gerontologist,
      15(1), 68-72.
Tenants in a renowned low-rent public housing project with special design features
for the elderly report satisfaction with their quarters at the end of their eighth
year in residence, leading to author's conclusion that improved housing can be a
major factor in bettering later years of life.

525   Donahue, W.T.; Thompson, M.M.; Curren, D.J. (Eds.) (1977). Congregate hous-
      ing for older people: An urgent need: A growing demand. Washington DC: US
      Department of Health, Education and Welfare (OHD) 77-20284. 221p.
Congregate housing described as encompassing many assisted living environments
for the physically, mentally, or socially impaired. Barriers in Federal housing and
social services programs identified; potential Federal and state sources of funding
discussed. Exceptional annotated bibliography.

526   Eckert, J.K. (1979). Urban renewal and redevelopment: High risk for the mar-
      ginally subsistent elderly. The Gerontologist, 19(5), 496-502.
First-hand observation for one year in a single room occupancy hotel in San Diego
CA, together with a health questionnaire, lead to conclusion that elderly in SROs
draw important support from fellow tenants and their own self-reliance. Urban
planners asked to consider social implications of redevelopment.

527   Greenstein, D. (1979). HUD researches elderly needs. Generations, 3(3),
      12-13.
A report by an analyst from the Department of Housing and Urban Development on
legislative authority provided for three important resarch projects completed by
1979 and a 10-year housing survey begun in 1978. Author poses policy issues
facing the Department relative to its programs for serving the elderly.

528   Harel, Z.; Harel, B.B. (1978). On-site coordinated services in age-segegated
      and age-integrated public housing. The Gerontologist, 18(2), 153-166.
Residence in age-segregated quarters is associated with higher levels of service
utilization, residential stability, and higher survival rates. Authors urge policymakers to provide for structural arrangements encouraging informal supports.

529   Heumann, L.F. (1978). Planning assisted independent living programs for the
      semi-independent elderly. The Gerontologist, 18(2), 145-152.
A two-year study leads to development of a descriptive model of "assisted independent living" useful to aging, regional, and housing planning agencies. Three sub-
models are provided, addressing housing and support service needs. Analytic tools
identify priority needs and coordinate service delivery.

530   Lane, T.S.; Feins, J.D. (1985). Are the elderly overhoused? Definitions of
      space utilization and policy implications. The Gerontologist, 25(3), 243-249.
Estimates that in 1980 6.9 million, or 35 percent of all elderly households, were

underutilizing living space. However, mobility among such homeowners is low, and vacated units that could house younger tenants are often unsuitable. Policymakers urged to design special, targeted programs.

531 Lawton, M.P. (1985). Housing and living environments of older people. In: Binstock, R.H.; Shanas, E. (Eds.). Handbook of aging and the social sciences. New York: Van Nostrand Reinhold Company, 450-478.
Final section admirably summarizes issues arising from varying housing needs of the elderly and the dwindling public policy response. The major need is "to remain in their homes in the community." Methods of uniting public, private effort need exploration; European examples cited. Outstanding references.

532 Lawton, M.P. (1985). The relevance of impairments to age targeting of housing assistance. The Gerontologist, 25(1), 31-34.
Age or income are seen as inadequate criteria for Federal public housing assistance. Particularly in a period of reduced funding, a better standard would consider disability and income. Practical difficulties of determining such a criteria are discussed and applied to existing programs.

533 Lawton, M.P. (1979). Research: What is its role in program decisions? Generations, 3(3), 8-9.
A brief but remarkably useful account of the "frequent close synchrony of research and programming," with due credit for housing pioneers who promoted breakthrough ideas that later underwent a "consolidation phase" validating and broadening fundamental principles. Federal programs used as examples.

534 Lawton, M.P.; Greenbaum, M.; Liebowitz, B. (1980). The lifespan of housing environments for the aging. The Gerontologist, 20(1), 56-64.
Increase in service needs for residents of two planned, Federally-assisted housing projects is examined over periods of 19 and 14 years, and decline in independence of tenants is documented. Must choose between preserving original purposes of housing in a "constant" environment, or making "accommodating" changes.

535 Lawton, M.P.; Hoover, S.L. (Eds.). (1981). Community housing choices for older Americans. New York: Springer Publishing Company, 326p.
Finds that existing programs are "too few, too capricious in coverage, lacking in technical expertise and poorly coordinated." Authors provide an overview of Federal efforts, research needs, minority difficulties, suburban problems, and housing-service gaps and alternatives.

536 Lawton, M.P.; Moss, M.; Grimes, M. (1985). The changing service needs of older tenants in planned housing. The Gerontologist, 25(3) 258-264.
Residents (N=494) in five Federally-assisted projects were assessed over 12-14 years; function declines measured. "Patchwork" response of community services to meet growing needs has occurred; authors predict marginally independent residents will outstrip funding availability, unless adequate service networks evolve.

537 Lawton, M.P.; Newcomer, R.J.; Byerts, T.O. (Eds.). (1976). Community planning for an aging society. New York: McGraw-Hill Book Company, 340p.
Primarily directed at area agency on aging and other planners confronted by housing shortcomings for widely varying elderly clienteles. Part II by guest authors has chapters on differing shelter needs, Federal housing programs for the elderly, zoning issues, and utilization and costs of alternative care settings.

538   Liebowitz, B. (1978). Implications of community housing for planning and policy. The Gerontologist, 18(2), 138-143.
A well-researched Philadelphia Geriatric Center project providing quarters for non-related individuals in former one-family, semi-detached homes is analyzed from the viewpoint of the administrator. Difficulties, including shortfalls in Federal support, discussed. An useful chart gives details on other projects.

539   Mayer, N.S.; Lee, O. (1981). Federal home repair programs and elderly home-owner's needs. The Gerontologist, 21(3), 312-322.
Assistance available from the Department of Housing and Urban Renewal, the Farmers Home Administration, and the Older Americans Act is analyzed, and older persons are found to receive less help than warranted. Funding cutbacks have since eroded such programs, but the author's discussion remains useful.

540   McConnell, S.R.; Usher, C.E. (1980). Intergenerational house-sharing: A research report and resource manual. Los Angeles: Andrus Gerontology Center, 52p.
Analysis of two house-sharing agencies (one in New York, the other in California) suggests many advantages and some disincentives. Possibilities of more widespread sharing discussed, but Federal policy deterrents in Section 8 Housing assistance, food stamps, and Supplemental Security Income are recognized.

541   McFarland, M.C. (1976). The emergence of a new concept—congregate housing for the elderly. Aging, Nos.256-257, 7-9.
Concise account of wavering Federal policy on providing supportive services to elderly residents in assisted housing, together with arguments for meeting the "desperate" congregate housing need. Note: The same author, on pp.14-15, summarizes points made at a significant congregate housing conference in 1975.

542   McGuire, M.C. (1969). The status of housing for the elderly. The Gerontologist, 9(1), 10-14.
The Assistant for Problems of the Elderly and Handicapped at the US Department of Housing and Urban Development gives a summary of ongoing programs and new initiatives as they stood in the final year of the Johnson Administration. Particularly useful for researchers tracing history of congregate and rural housing.

543   Montgomery, J.E.; Stubbs, A.C.; Day, S.S. (1980). The housing environment of the rural elderly. The Gerontologist, 20(4), 444-451.
Data collected as part of a five-year regional research project in 17 counties of nine states shows negligible use of Federal programs offering home improvement assistance. Most frequently sought help was from the Cooperative Extension Service. Researchers urged to seek answers.

544   Myers, P. (1979). Urban renovation and the elderly. Perspective on Aging, 8(3), 4-8.
A study by the Conservation Foundation finds that city renovation strategies in many cities need examination for their sometimes severe impact upon elderly residents, often through public/private partnership action. On the other hand, neighborhood conservation may hold new opportunities.

545   Nachison, J.S.; Leeds, M.H. (1983). Housing policy for older Americans in the
      1980s: An overview. Journal of Housing for the Elderly, 1(1), 3-13.
Identifies a "hard core," perhaps 8 percent of older Americans, in desperate need
of housing assistance, despite significant gains of prior decades. Gives pro and con
descriptions of housing vouchers, greater availability of housing with services, and
"cashing out" of welfare and related programs.

546   Newman, S.; Reschovsky, J.; Marans, R. (1985). Federal policy and the mobi-
      lity of older homeowners: The effects of the one-time capital gains exclusion.
      Ann Arbor: University of Michigan Institute for Social Research, 83p.
Effects of allowing up to $125,000 exclusion of capital gains on sale of a home
for sale of a home by an older homeowner are analyzed, using national survey of
households (N=5,000) of the Panel Study of Income Dynamics. Limited improvement
of homeowner mobility found. The exclusion is regarded as regressive.

547   Newman, S.J. (1985). Housing and long term care: The suitability of the
      elderly's housing to the provision of in-home services. The Gerontologist,
      25(1) 35-40.
Policymakers are urged to give due consideration of housing factors in meeting
growing demand for home care services. Available evidence, while inconclusive,
shows that a substantial group of elders likely to need such services are in environments that impede or preclude efficient delivery of them.

548   Newman, S.J. (1985). Housing policy for the elderly: The shape of things to
      come. Generations, 9(3), 14-17.
Identifies three major challenges: shaping and targeting assistance to elderly homeowners, overcoming geographic imbalances in housing need caused in part by migration, and adapting housing to meet long term care needs.

549   Newman, S.J.; Struyk, R.J. (1984). An alternative targeting strategy for
      housing assistance. The Gerontologist, 24(6), 584-592.
Suggests replacement of single-year income eligibility criteria with a permanence
of poverty standard. The 1978 (most recent) Annual Housing Survey and the Panel
Study of Income Dynamics provide information supporting the appropriateness,
administrative practicality, and fairness of this approach.

550   Niebanck, P.L.; Pope, J.B. (1965). The elderly in older urban areas: Problems
      of adaptation and the effects of relocation. University of Pennsylvania: In-
      stitute for Environmental Studies, 174p.
Finds that older residents were prominent among the 1.5 million persons involun-
tarily required during the prior 15 years to vacate their homes to make way for
urban renewal and other publicly supported projects. Cites governmental responsibility to help. A significant work, enhanced by an excellent bibliography.

551   President's Commission on Housing. (1982). Special housing problems of the
      elderly and handicapped. In: Foote, J. (Ed.). The report of the President's
      Commission on Housing. 49-56.
Established in June 1981, this Commission recognized housing as a national priority. Its recommendations recognize special needs of the frail elderly and endorse
mechanisms to enable older homeowners to convert home equity into income while
remaining in their homes.

552   Pritchard, D.C. (1983). The art of matchmaking: A case study in shared housing. The Gerontologist, 23(2), 174-179.
One year of experience in a small multi-purpose senior service aging (San Diego CA) reveals positive motivations for many older homeowners to share residences, but negative attitudes deter others. More adequate funding and staffing seen as needed for definitive findings on a potentially significant housing option.

553   Pynoos, J. (1984). Elderly housing politics and policy. Generations, 9(1), 26-30.
Portrays housing for the elderly as "a critical yet unappreciated societal issue." Traces early Federal successes and challenges of the 1980s. Calls for subsidies to continue at a reasonable level even as other options are invoked.

554   Rosow, I. (1960). Retirement housing and social integration. The Gerontologist, 1(2), 85-91.
An important challenge to a "firm ideological conviction" among many gerontologists that segregation of the elderly into housing settings is "undemocratic, invidious, and demoralizing." Finds that "re-integration of older people into new groups may facilitate their transition to a new aged role...".

555   Schulz, J.H. (1967). Some economics of aged home ownership. The Gerontologist, 7(1), 73-74, 80.
Analyzes ramifications of imputing a rent value for homes with elderly owners; warns that social policy implciations are not at all clear: "The fundamental economic question which an aged homeowner must consider is owning his present house costs less (budget-wise) than selling it..."

556   Struyk, R.J. (1985). Future housing assistance policy for the elderly. The Gerontologist, 25(1), 41-46
Long-standing shortcomings in developing well-rounded housing policy have been intensified by sharp program cutbacks in 1980s. Sharper targeting to low-income households is achieving greater equity, but additional steps are needed, including more congregate housing for the frail and practical assistance to homeowners.

557   Struyk, R.J. (1985). Housing-related needs of elderly Americans and possible Federal responses. Journal of Housing for the Elderly, 2(4), 3-23.
Foresees a new housing policy stressing that relationship of factors needed to maintain personal independence, with joint provision of housing and support services. Congress challenged to "rise above narrow committee jurisdictional issues to formulate an overall strategy."

558   Struyk, R.J.; Soldo, B.J. (1980). Improving the elderly's housing: A key to preserving the nation's housing stock and neighborhoods. Cambridge MA: Ballinger Publishing Company, 324p.
A stimulating mustering of data and arguments for bolstering current Federal programs with practical, coordinated efforts to improve housing for older persons living in the community, thus helping to revitalize communities.

559   Turner, M.A. (1985). Building housing for the low-income elderly: Cost containment in the Section 202 Program. The Gerontologist, 25(3), 271-277.
Cost containment measures viewed as undermining design and other unique features of the direct loan 202 program, under which nonprofit sponsors have frequently

provided high environmental and service standards. To restructure 202, its explicit goal should be to bridge the housing-institutional gap.

560   Urban Land Institute. (1983). Housing for a maturing population. Washington DC: Urban Land Institute, 246p.
Informative papers by authors who emphasize neglected areas of need in meeting housing needs of the elderly. Modification of existing stock, it is argued, requires more flexible governmental initiatives.

561   US House of Representatives. Select Committee on Aging, Subcommittee on Housing and Consumer Interests; US Senate, Special Committee on Aging. (1985). Home equity conversion: Issues and options for the elderly homeowner. SuDoc Y4.Ag4/2:H75/7, 97p.
A joint briefing offering papers updating issues related to home equity conversion including reverse mortgage insurance, sale leaseback arrangements and related tax issues. Especially useful is an overview by Ken Scholen of the National Center for Home Equity Conversion.

562   US Senate. Special Committee on Aging. (1978). Single room occupancy: A need for national concern. SuDoc Y4.Ag4/:S16, 57p.
Federal policies viewed as balking or destroying a housing option said to be suitable and desirable for many individuals, including large numbers of older persons. Positive examples of conversion or maintenance given, together with recommendations for policy changes. Informative appendices.

563   Zais, J.P.; Struyk, R.J.; Thibodeau, T. (1982). Housing assistance for older Americans: The Reagan prescription. Washington DC: Urban Institute, 125p.
Administration proposals for a drastic cutback in Federal housing support, relying on existing housing stock rather than new construction, discussed and compared to Congressional actions. A priority goal, to limit Federal housing to a fixed number of slots, analyzed for impact on older people. Extensive references.

SERVICES
COMMUNITY SERVICES

564   Bryant, E.S.; El-Attar, M. (1984). Migration and redistribution of the elderly: A challenge to community services. The Gerontologist, 24(6), 634-640.
Population restribution for 1960-70 and 1970-80 included three elderly migration patterns. Analysis indicates a lag in locating services in areas of expected demand. Research suggested to help policymakers and service providers. Definitive references.

565   Kamerman, S.B. (1976). Community services for the aged: The view from eight countries. The Gerontologist, 16(6), 529-537.
Support for the aged "in comfort and dignity, be it in their own home, another's home, or a special facility" is examined in the United States, Canada, Israel, and European nations. Significant variations exist in the countries, but a common core of "personal social services" is emerging.

566   Wood, J. (1985). Federal funding cutbacks hard on increasingly popular senior centers. Perspective on Aging, 14(5), 14-17.
Senior centers serving predominantly poor populations are said to face difficulties

in continuing service. Other findings by the Aging Health Policy Center reveal that in 1981-84 centers had staff reductions (but some gains in volunteers), subtle changes in programming, and modest new private funding.

567   US General Accounting Office. (1986). Community services: Block grant helps address local social service needs. GAO/HRD-86-91, 36p.
GAO investigators examined Community Services Block Grant (CSBG) operations in 16 community action agencies and 21 public social services agencies in eight states. In reply to Administration proposals that CSBG be terminated because its services are redundant, GAO reports local views of CSBG funds as essential.

LEGAL SERVICES

568   Bell, W.G.; Schmidt, W.; Miller, K. (1981). Public guardianship and the elderly: Findings from a national study. The Gerontologist, 21(2), 194-202.
Often relying on funding from Federal programs, states have established varying forms of protective services, which have as their avowed purpose the facilitation of independent living and avoidance of exploitation and abuse. This review of statutes in 34 states gives useful details.

569   Fretz, B.D. (1984). Legal services and the elderly poor. Generations, 8(3), 14-16.
Predicts that program cutbacks and economic problems will cause a need for more legal services, but points out substantial erosion of Federal resources to serve the legal needs of older poor people began in 1981. Discusses work of National Senior Citizens Law Center and policy-related challenges.

570   Regan, J.J. (1978). Intervention through adult protective services programs. The Gerontologist, 18(3), 250-253.
Spurred on by passage of the Title XX social services program in 1974, states established protective services intended to provide preventive, supportive, and surrogate services without excessive intervention. Author advances principles to protect client's rights, suggests amendment to adopt such principles.

571   Regan, J.J.; Springer, G. (1977). Protective services for the elderly. Washington DC: US Senate. Special Committee on Aging. SuDoc Y4.Ag4:Se6/10, 129p.

Estimates that 3 to 4 million elderly persons need some form of protective care or assistance, and notes that Federal programs frequently pay for such service. States, however, have more direct authority. Model statutes offered.

NUTRITION

572   Calasanti, T.M.; Hendricks, J. (1986). A sociological perspective on nutrition research among the elderly: Toward conceptual development. The Gerontologist, 26(3), 232-238.
Summarizes research on Federally-supported meal programs and reports conflicting findings on their usefulness to differing groups of older persons. An "overarching theoretical perspective" is called for to join diverse factors and provide a future research agenda.

573   Harel, Z. (1985). Nutrition site service users: Does racial background make a difference? The Gerontologist, 25(3), 286–291.
Interviews with 701 elderly participants in Older Amerians Act nutrition programs in five Ohio counties indicate no significant differences in service utilization by black and white consumers. However, blacks found to be considerably more disadvantaged in personal security, health and functional status, and access to benefits.

574   Hollonbeck, D.; Ohls, J.C. (1984). Participation among the elderly in the Food Stamp Program. The Gerontologist, 24(6), 616–621.
Interviews with 1,500 Food Stamp participants and 800 eligible, non-participating persons (in Oregon, South, Carolina, New York) suggest no single reason for low (approximately one-half) participation rate of older persons. Professionals advised on actions intended to help elders claim entitlement.

575   Howell, S.C. (1970). Applied research needs in nutrition and aging. The Gerontologist, 10(1), 73–75.
Criticizes frequent failure to reach elderly most in need of nutrition and other services and absence of systematic and continuous mechanisms to translate research for practitioners. Asks for implementation and evaluation research in demonstration, service programs.

576   Howell, S.C.; Loeb, M.B. (1969). Food services for the older adult. In: Nutrition and aging: A monograph for practitioners. The Gerontologist, 9(3), Pt. II. 75–86.
Useful to policy historians and nutrition researchers for details on Federally-assisted programs in place to meet varying needs, including Older Americans Act demonstration programs succeeded by a national congregate and home-delivered meals program. Appendix A discusses research and demonstration needs.

577   McGovern, G. (1976). Meals on wheels: Guidepost to the future. Perspective on Aging, 5(4), 11–13.
The Chairman of the US Senate Select Committee on Nutrition and Human Needs sees positive results from a broadened home-delivered meal program through the Older Americans Act. Meals on wheels regarded as "a near-perfect mechanism for transmitting information and referral services."

578   Nestle, M.; Lee, P.R.; Fullarton, J. (1983). Nutrition policy and the elderly. San Francisco: Aging Health Policy Center, University of California, 24p.
Examines Older Americans Act and other Federal programs intended to improve nutrition of the elderly; finds a lack of coordination that has placed them at severe disadvantage, despite tangible beneficial results from several of them. Gives recommendations for research, program modifications.

579   Schneider, R.L. (1979). Barriers to effective outreach in Title VII nutrition programs. The Gerontologist, 19(2). 163–68.
Interviews with directors of 15 Older American Act nutrition programs throughout Virginia identify barriers to full participation by the elderly. Detailed recommendations given; greater policy flexibility sought, including less emphasis on regular attendance.

580   US General Accounting Office. (1978). Actions needed to improve the nutri-
      tion program for the elderly. HRD-78-58, 35p.
Finds that the Older Americans Act meals program "has played a vital role in
addressing the social and nutritional needs," but needs closer attention to data
collection and other administrative problems.

OLDER AMERICANS ACT

581   Armour, P.K.; Estes, C.L.; Noble, M.L. (1981). The continuing design and
      implementation problems of a national policy on aging: Title III of the Older
      Americans Act. In: Hudson, R.B. (Ed.). The aging in politics: Process and
      policy. Springfield IL: Charles C. Thomas, 199-219.
Mixed legislative mandates regarded as diminishing effectiveness of state and area
agencies on aging. One consequence is a frequent inability to focus on the most
disadvantaged elderly. Another factor is decentralization, or delegation of essential
Federal responsibilities to the aging network.

582   Bechill, W.D. (1968). Some basic priorities in services for older Americans.
      Washington DC: US Administration on Aging. 16p.
The first US Commissioner of the Administration on Aging reports on two years of
experience with that agency. A key priority was to assist state agencies to "be as
strong and viable" as possible. Service priorities include: senior centers, employment, homemaker and supportive services, and nutrition.

583   Coberly, S.; et al. (1980). A policy note on the 1978 Amendments to the
      Older Americans Act. The Gerontologist, 20(2), 140-147.
An analysis of the potential consequences of 1978 legislation authorizing states to
designate as a planning and service area (for an area agency on aging) any unit of
general purpose local government having a population of 100,000 or more. Fiscal,
political, and administrative difficulties foreseen.

584   Cohen, E.S. (1979). Editorial: Squeezing the interstices. The Gerontologist,
      19(2), 130.
Heavy new responsibilities were laid upon the Older Americans Act in 1978 amendments, but this editorial finds Administration on Aging had fewer personnel in 1979
than in 1974. The ability of AoA to "map out and implement cogent research, education, and demonstration strategies" is questioned.

585   Coulter, O. (Ed.). (1975). AoA is focal point for Federal activities on aging.
      Aging, No.247, 12-22.
A detailed description of the history, structure, and objectives of the Administration on Aging as it implemented provisions of the 1973 Older Americans Act
amendments. The Office of State and Community programs is described as working
"to create broad services for aging."

586   Doolin, J. (1985). "America's Untouchables": The elderly homeless. Perspective
      on Aging, 9(2), 8-11.
Incomplete but convincing data indicates a substantial number of older persons are
among the homeless, who are categorized as chronic or traditional, deinstitutionalized, or new or temporary "dishoused." A Boston senior multiservice center
program to tap Older Americans Act group meals is described.

587   Estes, C.L. (1974). Community planning for the elderly: A study of goal dis-
      placement. Journal of Gerontology, 29(6), 684-691.
A two-year study of three planning organizations leads to findings that activities
overlapped, were largely symbolic and self-serving, and lacked hierarchical authority. Implications for the new Older Americans Act area agency on aging network
are discussed.

588   Federal Council on the Aging. (1981). Toward more effective implementation
      of the Older Americans Act: A staff report. GPO 0-720-019/4554, 116p.
A Congressionally-mandated study asks whether the Administration on Aging
approach is plausible in meeting problems and opportunities of 35 million Americans
aged 60 and over. Concludes that fundamental disagreements over underlying principles and strategies hamper effective service delivery and targeting.

589   Ficke, S.C. (1985). An orientation to the Older Americans Act. (Second edi-
      tion.) Washington DC: National Association of State Units on Aging. 122p.
This 20th anniversary appraisal describes the "network" of state and area agencies
on aging as "one of the most dynamic systems in human services today," and as a
key element in the "aging policy system." Detailed legislative history provided,
together with accounts of state and area agency responsibilities.

590   Ficke, S.C. (1982). State units on aging: Understanding their roles and re-
      sponsibilities. Washington DC: National Association of State Units on Aging,
      233p.
Gives a national overview of state agencies and "the partnerships they develop and
maintain with virtually every level of government, the private and voluntary sectors." Helpful historical background, statistical portrait of staffing and agency
functions. Extensive references, good bibliography.

591   Flemming, A.; Tolliver, L.M. (1983). Older Americans Act Title III proposed
      regulations: A public policy debate. Perspective on Aging, 12(5), 4-16.
An exchange of letters between National Council on the Aging President Flemming
and US Commissioner on Aging Tolliver airs differences arising from NCOA's concern about "very extensive changes proposed" in Older Americans Act policy. The
Commissioner cites Administration "intent to reduce regulatory burden and provide
state and area agencies with greater flexibility."

592   Fritz, D. (1979). The Administration on Aging as an advocate: Progress,
      problems, and perspectives. The Gerontologist, 19(2). 141-150.
AoA's advocacy role is regarded as slow in developing and perhaps overwhelmed by
AoA's program responsibilities. Suggestions for improvement include division of ad-
vocacy tasks with other Federal units, better use of research findings.

593   Gilbert, N.; Specht, H. (1979). Title XX planning by area agencies on aging:
      Efforts, outcomes and policy implications. The Gerontologist, 19(3), 264-274.
A questionnaire survey of 479 area agencies on aging indicates considerable opportunity existed in 1975 for access to funding under the Title XX social services
program. Two main paths of influence are efforts by the local area agencies and
action at the state level by the state unit on aging or related agencies.

594   Greenblatt, B.; Ernst, T. (1972). The Title III program: Field impressions and policy options. The Gerontologist, 12(2), 191-196.
A vigorous critique of the limited effectiveness of the Older Americans Act major funding source at an early stage in its development. Finds tokenism, inequality, and few innovations, based on an 18-state survey. A "social credit card" among proposed policy options. Indigenous control, clearer Federal mandates emphasized.

595   Hudson, R.B. (1974). Rational planning and organizational imperatives: Prospects for area planning in aging. In: Eisele, F.R. (Ed.). The political consequences of aging. The Annals of the American Academy of Political and Social Science. 415(September), 41-54.
Older Americans Act amendments of 1973, in a marked departure from prior policy, called for sub-state area agencies on aging. This early analysis predicts that national and area policy objectives are likely to differ and that the area agencies will be confronted with fundamental dilemmas.

596   National Association of Area Agencies on Aging. (1982). A profile of state and area agencies on aging: 1981. Washington DC: 25p.
Uses National Data Base on Aging to present characteristics, activities and services of state and area aging units. Describes placement of such agencies within governmental structures, staffing, individuals served, contracting providers, and funding. Finds that 26 percent of area agency budgets was non-Federal.

597   Nelson, G. (1980). Social services to the urban and rural aged: The experience of the area agencies on aging. The Gerontologist, 20(2), 200-207.
Rural area agencies on aging (under the Older Americans Act) are found to be deficient in funding and staffing for development of continuum care and other services for frail, at-risk elderly. It is proposed that minimum necessary funding levels be established, and that allocation formulas include rural factors.

598   Schulder, D. (1985). Older Americans Act a vast network of public, private agencies. Perspective on Aging, 14(5), 4-7.
Reviews modest beginnings and gradual development of the Older Americans Act on the 20th anniversary year of enactment. Describes a wide range of other concerns and programs being addressed by state and area agencies, providers, and private agencies.

599   US House of Representatives. Select Committee on Aging, Subcommittee on Human Services. (1984). Older Americans Act: A staff summary. Third Revision. SuDoc Y4.Ag4/2:0l1/984, 164p.
A sourcebook for legislative history and provisions, including the 1984 amendments. Interpretive commentary about implementation of the legislation is useful; excellent appendices detail program operations.

600   US Senate. Special Committee on Aging. Advisory Council. (1971). The Administration on Aging—or a successor? Committee Print, 38p.
An advisory unit, just before the 1971 White House Conference on Aging, issued this report, expressing concern about the perceived shortcomings and low status of the agency responsible for administering the Older Americans Act. Recommendation made for an independent agency.

SOCIAL SERVICES

601 Ahrens, R.J. (1976). Planning, providing, and coordinating services for Chicago's elderly. In: Bild, B.R.; Havighurst, R.J. Senior Citizens in Great Cities: The Case of Chicago. The Gerontologist, 16(1), Part 2. 80-85.
An account of almost 25 years in the evolution of a citywide agency tapping many funding sources and finally becoming an area agency on aging under the Older Americans Act. A Senior Central program to coordinate services and provide one-stop service is described in detail.

602 Alfaro, J.; Holmes, M. (1981). Caveats and cautions: Title XX group eligibility for the elderly. The Gerontologist, 21(4), 374-381.
In response to widespread criticism of the individual means test imposed when Title XX was implemented in 1975, Federal authority was given to states to establish eligibility criteria on a conditional group basis. Arguments for and against group eligibility are given.

603 Bild, B.R.; Havighurst, R.J. (1976). Knowledge and use of services. In: Senior citizens in great cities: The case of Chicago. The Gerontologist, 16(1), Part 2. 76-79.
Included in a broad survey, questions about services elicited the fact that only a reduced fare program enjoyed wide usage and knowledge among Chicago's elderly. Of 15 other programs examined, the least well known were Friendly Visitors, financial advice and emergency housing.

604 Dressel, P.L. (1982). Policy sources of worker dissatisfactions: The case of human services in aging. Social Service Review. 56(3). 406-423.
Focuses on four complaint areas: lack of resources, service agency problems, conflicts in mandates and rules, and certain client tendencies. Identifies dysfunctional public policy characteristics, including "calculated fragmentation" that intensify or cause such attitudes.

605 Gold, B.D. (1974). The role of the Federal Government in the provision of social services to older persons. In: Eisele, F.R. (Ed.). The political consequences of aging. The Annals of the American Academy of Political and Social Science. 415(September), 55-69.
Describes Federal support of social services as predominant because neither society nor the market system has responded to the needs of a growing aging population. Still, a complete range of services is available nowhere in the nation. Widely varying sources of services discussed; little liklihood seen for consolidated program.

606 Juarez and Associates. (1984). Alternative financing mechanisms: A synthesis of issues and findings. US Department of Health and Human Services, Office of Human Development Services. 39p.
A summary of OHDS and other research and demonstration projects to test financing of human services through vouchers, cash subsidies, tax credits, and user fees. Frequent references to older persons. "Empowerment" hypothesis examined. Project summaries of OHDS projects; brief but useful bibliography.

607 Kahn, A.J.; Kamerman, S.B. (1978). The course of "personal social services." Public Welfare, 36(3), 29-42.
An appraisal, during the early years of the Title XX social service program, of

progress being made in developing a core of essential services. Categorical approach in other areas recognized as an important stopgap, but also as a force for fragmentation and inadequacy.

608   Krout, J.A. (1983). Knowledge and use of services by the elderly: A critical review of the literature. International Journal of Aging and Human Development, 17(2), 153-167.
Finds that knowledge of and attitudes toward services for the elderly are "not overwhelmingly positive," and that the rate of use is even more negative. No consistent profile of service users emerges from the literature; existing research criticized as largely atheoretical. Useful references.

609   McCaslin, R. (1981). Next steps in information and referral for the elderly. The Gerontologist, 21(2), 184-193.
Twenty-five years of discussion about I&R needs have produced little empirical findings, despite an Older Americans Act mandate that clients should have access to such services. Researchable projects presented; social policymakers urged to turn more attention to issue. Excellent search of literature and references.

610   Mathiasen, G. (1970). The golden years: A tarnished myth. Washington DC: National Council on the Aging, 157p.
Presents findings from the first major survey of older poor Americans, in which 50,000 persons at 12 demonstration projects were interviewed. More than 28,000 referrals were made to agencies or services, but in 24,000 other cases, services did not exist. Many poor persons did not claim Social Security benefits.

611   Nelson, G. (1982). A role for Title XX in the aging network. The Gerontologist, 22(1), 18-25.
Using 1977 data on use of the Title XX Social Services program (later the Social Services Block Grant), author finds that Title XX expenditures for the elderly as large or larger than amounts then available under Older Americans Act. Development of multiple criteria of need is suggested.

612   Schram, S.F. (1981). Elderly policy particularism and the new social services. In: Hudson, R.B. (Ed.). The aging in politics: Process and policy. Springfield IL: Charles C. Thomas, 199-219.
Limited evidence suggests the elderly are not faring well in the Title XX social services program for low-income persons of all ages. Anti-discrimination actions regarded as unpromising because of strains with other generations. Universalistic and particularistic approaches analyzed.

613   Silverstein, N.M. (1984). Informing the elderly about public services: The relationship between sources of knowledge and service utilization. The Gerontologist, 24(1), 37-40.
Information on elderly's utilization of 17 public services in Boston obtained from 706 household interviewees; fewer than one-quarter exhibited high level of social awareness. Author recommends against establishment of additional information and referral centers, urges more consumer participation in strategy meetings.

614   Stanfield, R.L. (1978). Services for the elderly: A catch-22. In: Hubbard, J.P. (Ed.). The economics of aging: The economic, political and social implications of growing old in America: Issues book, Washington DC: The National Journal, 12-15.
Summarizes problems arising from fragmentation of Federal services. Older Americans Act coordination goals cited, but Congress said to "legislate coordination with one hand while adding to the confusion with the other."

615   Tobin, S.S. (1975). Social and health services for the future aged. The Gerontologist, 15(1), Pt. II, 32-36.
Given sufficient funding and policy direction, social/health services are likely to include community-based organizations to integrate a wide range of services, smaller long term care institutions, and hospices. Warns: "...only through efficient linkages will there be a fit between changing needs and services."

616   Wood, J. (1983). Hidden implications for elders in the switch to private funding. Generations, 7(4), 30-31, 64.
Availability of community-based services to prevent unnecessary institutionalization viewed as especially vulnerable to dislocations caused by diminished Federal support: "To defund services is to defund agencies; in the case of social services, a significant number of nonprofit agencies are potentially at risk."

TRANSPORTATION

617   Bell, W.G.; Revis, J.S. (1983). Transportation for older Americans: Issues and options for the decade of the 1980s. US Department of Transportation, DOT I-83-42, 58p.
Updates earlier studies; incorporates material and recommendations from the 1980 Mini-Conference; finds that much progress has been made since 1970, but that new needs arise with the growth of frail elderly. Directed primarily at state and local officials, it urges use of important, if limited, Federal resources.

618   Bell, W.G.; Olsen, W.T. (1974). An overview of public transportation for the elderly: New directions for social policy. The Gerontologist, 14(4), 324-330.
Finds that most "solutions" for transit-dependent groups are "fragmentary, simplistic, inefficient, and impermanent." Provides a useful summary of Federal and other programs and cites deficiencies. Asks for a genuine national policy, reaffirming of the social nature of urban mass transit.

619   Faris, J.B. (Ed.). (1977). Section 504: Impact on AoA Programs. Aging, Nos. 275-276, 14-16.
Discusses section of Rehabilitation Act of 1973 intended to end discrimination among the handicapped, including about 7 million elderly, with special reference to transportation services. Administration on Aging program directors alerted to other regulatory requirements specified in April 1977.

620   Matthews, S.H. (1982). Participation of the elderly in a transportation system. The Gerontologist, 22(1), 26-31.
A state office on aging grant provided startup funds for a rural elderly, eight-county transportation system "enmeshed in a philosophy familiar to persons involved in rural cooperatives." An underlying principle was "participation with power." Conflicting requirements of three Federal programs cause severe erosion.

621   Stirner, F.W. (1978). The transportation needs of the elderly in a large urban environment. The Gerontologist, 18(12), 207-271.
A questionnaire (N=1,129) transportation needs survey in Philadelphia reveals: 30 percent of the elderly need transportation, 40 percent are handicapped and 6 percent are wheelchair bound. Author concludes that overall transportation needs of the elderly are not being met.

622   US Senate. Special Committee on Aging. (1970). Older Americans and transportation: A crisis in mobility. Committee Report, 113p.
A distillation from many sources including Committee hearings documenting transportation difficulties that "are intensifying many other difficult problems faced by the elderly..." Examples of positive action given.

CONSUMER ISSUES

623   Cooper, S. (1981). Fuel bills and the elderly. Aging, Nos.315-316. 11-14.
A useful review of the often extreme consequences of rising fuel bills on the elderly and the origins and extent of Federal, state, and private programs intended to provide partial relief. Consumer ignorance of such programs seen as a major problem.

624   Ducovny, A.M. (1969). The billion $ swindle: Frauds against the elderly. New York: Fleet Press Corporation, 242p.
Gaps in Federal policy recounted in chapters on quackery, therapeutic and prosthetic devices, mail order schemes, funeral arrangements, questionable nursing homes, Social Security imposters and con games. The government's role in educating the consumer discussed. Foreword gives other legislative proposals.

625   Faris, J.B. (Ed.). (1979). Elderly exploited in selling of Medigap coverage. Aging, Nos.295-296, p.2-5.
A review of Congressional, Federal Trade Commission, and individual studies raising questions about costs and effectiveness of some private policies sold to supplement Medicare coverage. Health Care Financing Administration public information efforts described. Federal and state legislation cited.

626   Liang, J.; Sengstock, M.C. (1981). The risk of personal victimization among the aged. Journal of Gerontology, 36(4), 463-471.
Analysis of the 1973-76 National Crime Survey reveals wide variations in victimization rates for elderly crime victims, related to size of community, marital status, sex and race. Findings suggest that crime prevention programs should be targeted at high risk groups.

627   Malinchak, A.A.; Wright, D. (1978). Older Americans and crime: The scope of elderly victimization. Aging, Nos.281-282. 11-16.
Informative, far-ranging distillation of research data, Congressional findings, and individual case studies. The Law Enforcement Assistance Administration criticized for significant fact-finding gaps. Elderly vulnerability to crime seen increased by economic, physical, environmental, and social factors.

628   McGhee, J.L. (1983). The vulnerability of elderly consumers. International Journal of Aging and Human Development, 17(3), 223-243.
An extensive research review identifies factors that may make the elderly more

vulnerable than younger persons to consumer fraud. Suggests that consumer policy would benefit from closer researcher attention to effects of age, cohort, and period on changes in attitudes and patterns of consumer behavior.

629   US Congress. Office of Technology Assessment. (1985). Medications and the elderly. In: Technology and aging in America. Washington DC: OTA-BA-264, 137-147.
Problems involved in drug treatment of older persons described, including biologic age differences in drug effects and metabolism and need for increased education of health care providers and consumers. Suggested Congressional issues and options deal with drug testing, costs of drug development, and education.

630   US House of Representatives. Select Committee on Aging. (1984). Quackery: A $10 billion scandal. SuDoc Y4.Ag4/2:Q2, 250p.
Declares "The modern quack's prime target is the senior citizen," and recommends regulatory, legislative, and public educational actions needed to cope with fraud and consumer misconceptions.

631   US Senate. Special Committee on Aging. (1982). Fraud, waste and abuse in the Medicare pacemaker industry. SuDoc Y4.Ag4:M46/13, 207p.
An intensive investigation leads to conclusions that Medicare, which pays 80 to 90 percent of all pacemaker procedures in this country, is victimized by unreasonable costs, unnecessary prescriptions and utilization, defective warranties, inadequate monitoring, and other problems.

632   US Senate. Special Committee on Aging. (1965). Frauds and deceptions affecting the elderly: Investigations, findings, and recommendations: 1964. Committee Print. 73p.
Culminates an extensive investigation of health frauds and quackery, deceptive health insurance sales, interstate mail order sales, and pre-need burial services. Declares that the elderly are "the major victims of the highly-organized, high-pressure techniques of the modern day medicine man."

633   Wegner, F. (1983). Generics: The economics of prescriptions and the elderly. Generations, 8(2), 49-50.
Describes Federal and state policy actions that have eased or complicated increased prescribing of lower priced generic drugs. Consumer confidence viewed as gradually increasing, and "the good things promised about generic substitution are gradually happening, albeit slowly."

DISCRIMINATION

634   Eglit, H. (1985). Age and the law. In: Binstock, R.H.; Shanas, E. (Eds.). Handbook of aging and the social sciences. New York: Van Nostrand Reinhold Company, 528-553.
A useful review of significant US legal developments, including court decisions, related to rejection of age discrimination in Federal programs and in employment. Although the movement to reject age discrimination is gathering strength, analysis of judicial and legislative redress still finds ambivalence.

635   Grunewald, R.J. (1972). The Age Discrimination in Employment Act of 1967. Industrial Gerontology, No. 15, 1-11.
An Assistant Secretary of Labor summarizes early departmental actions, including a 1965 declaration that older worker unemployment was costing the economy an estimated one million man-years of productive time annually. Describes goal "to develop a national conscience about the effects of age discrimination...".

636   King, C.S. (1984). We need a national coalition on age discrimination. 50 Plus, 24(7), 10-11.
The widow of Martin Luther King Jr. warns of "massive economic insecurity" among the elderly, caused partially by age discrimination. She also criticizes negative policies affecting children and young adults, including a proposed subminimum wage that will then be "proposed for senior citizens."

637   Lester, R.A. (1981). Age, performance, and retirement legislation. In: Somers, A.R.; Fabian, D.R. (Eds.). The geriatric imperative: An introduction to gerontology and clinical geriatrics. New York, Appleton-Century-Crofts, 77-87.
Examines exemptions provided in the 1978 amendments to the Age Discrimination Act for tenured university faculty members and key business executives. Concludes that the executive exemption should be continued without change and that the faculty exemption should be extended, preferably for an indefinite period.

638   Morrison, M.H. (1981). ADEA and the future of retirement. Aging and Work, 4(4), 253-257.
Reports few immediate effects of 1978 Age Discrimination in Employment (ADEA) amendments, but notes growing employer interest in the changing workforce composition. Urges linkages among employment/retirement policies.

639   National Association of Office Workers. (1980). Vanished dreams: Age discrimination and the older woman worker. Cleveland OH: 30p.
Based on a nationwide survey of older women workers, consultation with the Equal Employment Opportunity Commission, and other research. Recommendations include upgraded enforcement of the Age Discrimination in Employment Act, improved pension coverage, and more job redesign.

640   US Commission on Civil Rights. (1977). The age discrimination study. Washington DC: GPO 733-0353/190. 112p.
Reports on a study of Federal programs: Community mental health centers, legal services, basic vocational rehabilitation, community health centers, Title XX social services, employment training, Medicaid, vocational education, and adult education. Concludes that age discrimination exists to some extent in each.

EDUCATION

641   Grabowski, S.M. (1980). Education and public policy for older adults. In: Markson, E.W.; Batra, G.R. (Eds.). Public policies for an aging population. Lexington MA: Lexington Books, 81-91.
Barriers to educational opportunity are described, despite "slight push" given by the 1971 White House Conference on Aging. Supportive services and outreach required, along with education. Confusion about aging said to exist in school curricula at all levels. Federal overemphasis on vocational requirements criticized.

642   Jacobs, B. (1985). Are we disenfranchising nine million elderly citizens? Per-
       spective on Aging, 14(3), 15-16.
Nine million "functionally illiterate" 55+ Americans are unable to understand
essential information or make informed choices. The US Department of Education
and other agencies are meeting some needs, as are state programs, but a National
Council on the Aging study finds shortcomings affecting older persons.

643   McClusky, H.Y. (1978). Designs for learning. In: Jarvik, L. (Ed.). Aging into
       the 21st Century: Middle-agers today. New York: Gardner Press, Inc. 169-
       184.
A stimulating prediction that by the year 2000 lifelong learning will have become
thoroughly accepted, helped along by policy and social change. Area agencies on
aging and congregate housing will help effect far-reaching change. Women's pre-
retirement training to become major new factor.

644   Moody, H.R. (1986). Education as a lifelong process. In: Pifer, A.; Bronte,
       L.(Eds.). Our aging society: Paradox and promise. New York: W.W. Norton,
       199-217.
Asks for national policy to recognize that increased longevity means an abundance
of life in later years with a potential for continued social productivity. Education
for the older adult also seen as a necessity for maintenance of society and to
promote self help, other new norms of social participation.

645   Morris, R.; Bass, S.A. (1986). The elderly as surplus people: Is there a role
       for higher education? The Gerontologist, 26(1), 12-17.
Gives rationale for developing a secondary labor market employing older people in
work designed neither to exploit older workers nor displace younger ones, primarily
in an expanded human service delivery system. Massachusetts pilot training program
described. Federal policy changes proposed.

646   Ossofsky, J. (1976). Nourishing the minds of the aging. In: Gross, R.; Gross,
       B.; Seidman, S. The new old: Struggling for decent aging. Garden City NY:
       Anchor Books. 257-266.
Governmental support for intellectual pursuits of the elderly viewed as an essential
function, even though other public policy goals on aging have not yet been met.
Statistics on educational activity by older persons given; negative attitudes
challenged; educational institutions urged to re-examine assumptions and programs.

647   Striner, H.E. (1972). Continuing education as a national capital investment.
       Washington DC: W.E. Upjohn Institute, 202p.
Adult education is viewed as facilitating transformation of the entire education
system, giving the individual lifetime skills. Comparisons made with European projects. Calls for a permanent education and training law for every worker over the
age of 17.

648   Stub, H.R. (1982.). Education and long life. In: Stub, H.R. The social conse-
       quences of long life. Springfield IL: Charles C. Thomas Publisher, 161-179.
Refers to Federal programs intended to make educational opportunity more
available in later years. Discusses a Lifelong Learning Act advanced by Senator
Walter Mondale in 1976. One provision called for a US Office of Lifetime
Learning.

EMPOWERMENT

649   Binstock, R.H. (1974). Aging and the future of American politics. In: Eisele,
       F.R. (Ed.). The political consequences of aging. The Annals of the American
       Academy of Political and Social Science. 415(September), 199–212.
Foresees little likelihood that the elderly will gain power by voting more cohesi-
vely in the future. The question will be whether government responds adequately
and appropriately to service and other needs of a rapidly growing segment of the
population.

650   Estes, C.L. (1973). Barriers to effective community planning for the elderly.
       The Gerontologist, 13(2), 178–183.
A study of four community planning organizations provides supporting evidence of
the argument that professionals often are resistant to direct participation by
elders in all phases of the planning process. Specific recommendations made to
involve the elderly in defining problems and planning strategies to deal with them.

651   Gallant, R.V.; Cohen, C.; Wolff, T. (1985). Changes of older persons' image,
       impact on public policy result from Highland Valley empowerment plan. Per-
       spective on Aging, 14(5), 9–13.
A Massachusetts area agency/home care corporation moves away "from the concept
of turning people into clients" and uses Older Americans Act and other funding to
enlist older persons as "an entitled group capable of shaping and offering resources" in several health programs, support, and consumer programs.

652   Hanna, W.J. (1981). Advocacy and the elderly. In: Davis, R.H. (Ed.).   Aging:
       Prospects and issues, Third Edition. Los Angeles: University of Southern Cal-
       ifornia Press. 297–310.
Emphasizes participation of older persons in many forms of program-related advocacy, including community groups, boards and local commissioners, state housing
agencies, area agencies on aging advisory boards, and coalitions.

FAMILY POLICY

653   Brody, S.J.; Poulshock, S.W.; Masciocchi, C.F. (1978). The family caring unit:
       A major consideration in the long-term support system. The Gerontologist,
       18(6), 556–561.
Family support is found to be a key factor determining why some persons are
institutionalized and score well on a functional disability measure, whereas others
scoring poorly are able to remain in the community. It is suggested that support of
the family caring unit should become a critical policy consideration.

654   Callahan, D. (1985). What do children owe elderly parents? The Hastings
       Center Report, 15(2), 32–37.
Reviews traditional moral obligations of children toward the welfare of their
elderly parents in light of official statements that states may require children to
pay part of Medicaid costs for parents' care. Includes useful summary of state
statutes.

655   Cantor, M. (1985). Families: A basic source of long term care for the elder-
       ly. Aging, No.349, 8–13.
Regards both informal and formal social care as valuable and urges care to avoid

upsetting the delicate balance between the two subsystems. Direct or indirect financial incentives may not be helpful to frail elderly. Notes that at least one-third of elderly are childless.

656 Fengler, A.P.; Goodrich, N. (1979). Wives of elderly disabled men: The hidden patients. The Gerontologist, 19(2), 175-183.
Interviews with married couples (N=34) show a close correlation in husband's and caregiving wife's morale. Wives with low morale are particularly in need of support. Financial assistance paid directly to families regarded as "a humane and economically justifiable policy for government to follow."

657 Goldwater, B. (1961). Family life and older persons. In: US Department of Health, Education, and Welfare. Aging with a future. 10-17.
An Arizona Senator, in a discussion paper prepared for the White House Conference on Aging, questions "those who feel that only through the intervention of a bureaucratic central government can the aged and their problems be helped." Argues for family, church, and local government responsibility.

658 Hareven, T. (1986). Life-course transitions and kin assistance in old age: A cohort comparison. In: Van Tassel, D.; Stearns, P.N. (Eds.). Old age in a bureaucratic society: The elderly, the experts, and the state in American history. New York: Greenwood Press, 110-126.
Historical precedents and attitudes persist among contemporary families in support and care of older members. Author warns against "romanticizing kin relations, particularly against the attempt to transfer responsibility for the elderly back to the family without adequate governmental assistance."

659 Maddox, G.L.; Siegler, I.C.; Blazer, D.G. (Eds.). (1980). Families and older persons: Policy, research, and practice. Durham NC: Duke University Center for the Study of Aging and Human Development, 198p.
Chapter nine cites papers from a national conference giving Executive Branch, historians', anthropological, Congressional, and academic views of policy formation and families of older people. Policy research discussed in final chapter.

660 Mindel, C.H. (1979). Multi-generational family households: Recent trends and implications for the future. The Gerontologist, 19(5), 456-463.
Argues for support of multigenerational households, perhaps through training of family members to provide certain medical care and services: "It is only by recognizing the degree of integration between the elderly and their family and other groups that coherent and socially useful policies can be developed."

661 New York State Office for the Aging. (1983). Family caregiving and the elderly: Policy recommendations and research findings. Albany: 71p.
A valuable compendium of research findings and analysis of shortcomings in Federal and other public programs. Recommendations are intended to offer a comprehensive research-based framework for future public action, and to help families to keep older members at home. Excellent bibliography.

662 Seltzer, M.M.; Troll, L.E. (1982). Conflicting public attitudes toward filial responsibility. Generations, 7(2), 26-27, 40.
Prevailing winds of conservatism and liberalism often alter expectations of family caregiving responsibility. Authors point out that practitioners are often caught in

the middle as attitudes range "between believing the Federal Government should provide everything and believing that it should do nothing."

663   Shanas, E. (1979). The family as a social support system in old age. The
      Gerontologist, 19(2), 169-174.
Data from the author's 1975 national survey indicate the major role of immediate family in providing social support in time of illness, often making it possible for bedfast persons to live outside institutions. To perform this function, families may need modified links with bureaucratic institutions.

664   Shanas, E.; Sussman, M.B. (1977). Comparative analyses and problematics In:
      Shanas, E.; Sussman, M.B. (Eds.) Family, bureaucracy, and the elderly. Durham
      NC: Duke University Press. 215-225.
Shared functions of the family and bureaucracies have become commonplace and may strengthen family structure by relieving younger generations of much responsibility for economic support and health care for the elderly. Bureaucracy regarded by authors as well-suited for uniform tasks, but must avoid elitism.

665   Stephens, R.C.; Blau, Z.S.; Oser, G.T.; Millar, M.D. (1978). Aging, social sup-
      port systems, and social policy. Journal of Gerontological Social Work. 1(1).
      33-45.
A Texas survey (2,672 respondents) shows that most aging persons have social supports. Persons most in need of such services (the poor, Mexican-Americans, and 70+) are least likely to call for them. Responsive social policies called for.

666   Sussman, M.B. (1985). The family life of old people. In: Binstock, R.H.;
      Shanas, E. (Eds.). Handbook of aging and the social sciences. New York: Van
      Nostrand Reinhold Company, 415-449.
The "New Federalism" in the United States and similar trends in other nations are reducing governments' willingness to develop and organize services for the elderly. Family networks can respond positively, often in cooperation with public programs. Extensive references.

667   Tobin, S.S.; Kulys, R. (1980). The family and services. In: Annual review of
      gerontology and geriatrics. Vol.I. Springer Publishing Company, 370-399.
Reviews the family as a resource, caregiving by families, the family and institutionalization, and the need for a Federal policy on families and aging. Outstanding references.

668   Weeks, J.R.; Cuellar, J.B. (1981). The role of family members in the helping
      networks of older people. The Gerontologist, 21(4). 388-394.
Interviewees (N=1139) representing 10 different ethnic groups in San Diego County CA report that immigrants are more likely than native-born elders to have family members help when in of need. At a time when publicly funded services may be dwindling, policymakers should tactfully strengthen natural support systems.

INTERGENERATIONAL CONCERNS

669   Kingson, E.R.; Hirshorn, B.A.; Harootyan, L.K. (1986). The common stake: The interdependence of generations. Washington DC: Gerontological Society of America, 30p.
Conflict among generations may be caused by misunderstandings and competitive attitudes. This study questions the intergenerational inequity conceptual framework and argues for full understanding of interdependence themes.

670   Kreps, J. (1977). Intergenerational transfers and the bureaucracy. In: Shanas, E.; Sussman, M.B. (Eds.) Family, bureaucracy, and the elderly. Durham NC: Duke University Press. 21-34.
Have shifts to intergenerational (as opposed to intrafamily) support resulted in conflicts of interest that set generations against each other? A tentative "no" answer is given. Does removal of income allocation issue improve family relations? Families can be stronger by intervening for older members.

671   Neugarten, B.L. (1970). The old and the young in modern societies. In: Shanas, E. (Ed.). Aging in contemporary society. Beverly Hills: Sage Publications, 13-24.
Foresees that a struggle for age rights could result in greater tensions among generations or in greater freedom. Older persons may become more vocal and add to intergenerational disputes, or they may become "younger" in outlook and objectives and therefore more accepted.

672   Wynne, E.A. (1986). Will the young support the old? In: Pifer, A.; Bronte, L. Our aging society: Paradox and promise. New York: W.W. Norton, 241-261.
Seemingly ingrained principles of reciprocity under which societal groups and family members recognize and act upon obligations often informally expressed and accepted will be put to increasing strain as the baby dearth generation follows the baby boomers. Strategies directed at attitudinal change discussed.

673   US House of Representatives. Select Committee on Aging. (1986). Protecting America's aged, children, and poor: Multigenerational needs, multigenerational solutions. SuDoc Y4.Ag4/2:A64/14, 55p.
Statements made at a forum held in conjunction with an annual meeting of the American Public Health Association are intended to help "dispel the notion of intergenerational conflict...". Appendices include an updated Committee analysis of Gramm-Rudman budget procedures on programs for the aged, children, and poor.

MINORITIES

674   Aguirre, B.E.; Bigelow, A. (1983). The aged in Hispanic groups: A review. International Journal of Aging and Human Development, 17(3), 177-201.
An inventory of social science reports about Mexican, Puerto Rican, and Cuban sub-national groups of elderly in the United States. Finds that Cuban and Puerto Rican elders have been largely disregarded, and that major gaps still exist in identifying factors affecting service use. Outstanding references.

675   Benitez, R. (1977). Ethnicity, social policy, and aging. In: Davis, R.H. (Ed.).
       Aging: Prospects and issues. (Revised, Fourth Printing). Los Angeles: Andrus
       Gerontology Center, 164-177.
Factors affecting minority aged include the special history each minority has in
relation to the American social system, stereotypes arising largely from work roles,
language or other differences arising in varying sub-cultures, and life experience
differences among young and older generations.

676   Chunn, J. (1978). The black aged and social policy. Aging, Nos.287-288,
       10-14.
Raises questions about social policies that do not adequately meet needs of elderly
blacks or, in some cases, work against their interests and well-being. A call is
made for a more adequate level of income and services, particularly health care
and housing, provided equitably.

677   Curley, L. (1982). Indian elders: A failure of aging policy. Generations, 6(3),
       28, 52.
Declares that older Indians are being especially underserved with respect to their
transportation, legal, homemaker/chore, employment and remedial training needs.
Gives a useful summary of demographic and other information provided by two
studies of the National Indian Council on Aging.

678   Fandetti, D.V.: Gelfand, D.E. (1976). Care of the aged: Attitudes of white
       ethnic families. The Gerontologist, 16(6), 544-549.
A Baltimore sample (N=100) reports a clear preference for family care of the
ambulatory aged and traditional institutions such as the church for long term care.
Social planners asked to determine whether pluralistic service delivery systems will
facilitate utilization of social services for the elderly.

679   Fuji, S.M. (1980). Minority group elderly: Demographic characteristics and
       implications for public policy. In: Annual Review of Gerontology and Geria-
       trics, Vol.I. New York: Springer Publishing Company, 261-284.
Gives a framework of information about "inequities the minority have endured as
victims of racism, ageism, and social and economic privation," and requests that
public policy pay due regard to cultural backgrounds and ethnic/racial differences,
emphasizing affirmative, corrective action.

680   Gelfand, D.E. (1982). Aging: The ethnic factor. Boston: Little, Brown and
       Company. 113p.
Origins of ethnic groups in the United States are examined. Ethnicity-related factors affecting use of public service programs include: lack of knowledge about
other cultures, unfamiliarity with existing services, low expectations of services,
and desire to maintain ethnic culture.

681   Gibson, R.C. (1986). Outlook for the black family. In: Pifer, A.; Bronte, L.
       (Eds.). Our aging society: Paradox and promise. New York: W.W. Norton,
       181-197.
Pinpoints issues of crucial concern: The most rapidly growing group of black
elderly are 80-plus women; the young outnumber of old in the black population,
and 50 percent of black children live in poverty yet will be expected to assume
proportionately more responsibility for supporting dependent elders.

288   Buchanan, J.; Haga, M.V.; Margolis, R.J. (1984). Health care USA: 1984—A citizens' prescription for reforming America's ailing health care system. Vol.I. Washington DC: The National Citizens' Board of Inquiry into Health in America, 34p.
Based on hearings in ten cities and related studies, this report makes "an urgent call for prompt enactment of a universal comprehensive national health care plan" for all age groups. It also makes specific recommendations for improvements in Medicare and Medicaid, and home health and other long term care.

289   Butler, R.N. (1986). How to create effective care spectrum? 'Money is there' for needed health system reforms. Perspective on Aging, 15(3), 4-6.
Criticizes "an essential failure in the American health enterprise to adapt to the demographic revolution we are now experiencing." Medicare called "antigeriatric" because of its emphasis on acute care. A community-based spectrum of care, it is argued, can be financed through systems reform, excise taxes.

290   Cantor, M.; Mayer, M. (1976). Health and the inner city elderly. The Gerontologist, 16(1), 17-24.
A sample (N=1,552) of 60-plus persons in the 26 poorest neighborhoods in New York City finds concern about health care prevalent even though most respondents report at least fair health and low hospitalization. Barriers to health care include lack of money and skepticism about doctors' effectiveness.

291   Davis, K. (1986). Paying the health-care bills of an aging population. In: Pifer, A.; Bronte, L. (Eds.) Our aging society: Paradox and promise. New York: W.W. Norton, 299-318.
A fundamental difficulty is lack of an explicit mechanism for controlling of health care resources. A prospective payment system for Medicare starting in 1983 has helped control costs, but is limited and needs improvement.

292   Davis, K. (1985). Health care policies and the aged: Observations from the United States. In: Binstock, R.H.; Shanas, E. (Eds.). Handbook of aging and the social sciences. New York: Van Nostrand Reinhold Company, 727-744.
A "rationale for public policy action" poses three principles: To maintain minimum standards of human decency, to repay past contributions to society, and to correct the failures of the private market. Future policy must offer health maintenance for younger people and develop adequate long term care for frail aged.

293   Ehrlich, P. (1983). Elderly health advocacy group: An integrative planning model of elderly consumers and service deliverers. The Gerontologist, 23(6), 569-72.
The Union County (IL) Elderly Health Advocacy Group (UCEHAG) is depicted as a consensus model for community health care planning and evaluation. Elderly consumers comprise more than 50 percent of membership. Positive response suggests viability of the model, especially in an era of Federal block grants.

294   Eisdorfer, C. (1976). Issues in health planning for the aged. The Gerontologist, 16(1), 12-16.
A brief but informative summary of ingrown problems affecting health care of the elderly, worth comparing to the situation existing a decade later. Topics include: Sparse integration of social and health services, prevention vs. care, the tendency for care to follow funding dollar, and dwindling support for training programs.

295 Estes, C.L.; Gerard, L.E.; Zones, J.S.; Swan, J.H. (1984). Political economy, health, and aging. Boston: Little, Brown & Co., 138p.
A detailed theoretical and factual critique of "the growing acceptance of the competitive ideology in health," and the consequences of this trend upon older Americans. Challenges the belief that care for the aged is a major factor to the health financing crisis. Extensive bibliography.

296 German, P.S.; Shapiro, S.; Chase, G.A.; Vollmer, M.H. (1978). Health care of the elderly in a medically disadvantaged population. The Gerontologist, 18(6), 547-555.
A survey of 718 65+ persons in two of three disadvantaged sections of Baltimore finds ready health care access for serious conditions, but limited availability for treatment of less serious but potentially disabling conditions. In the third, a health maintenance organization has had more success.

297 Gibson, D.E. (1984). Hospice: Morality and economics. The Gerontologist, 24(1), 4-7.
Questions legislative rationale for establishing Medicare coverage of hospice treatment for the dying. Charges that economic factors, rather than "alleged" humanitarian superiority of hospice care, have assumed primary importance.

298 Graber, J.B. (1970). Community health services. In: Hoffman, A.M. The Daily Needs and Interests of Older People. Springfield IL: Charles C. Thomas, 357-379.
Historically interesting review of Federal programs then serving health needs of the elderly and others. A Public Health Service viewpoint prevails, and PHS is described as having primary responsibility for the health protection of all persons. Home health care and other services discussed.

299 Graber, J.B. (1966). Findings and implications of a nationwide program review of resources available to meet the health needs of the aging and aged. The Gerontologist, 6(4), 191-200.
Important summary for researchers on history of health care policy. Springs from the Gerontology Branch of the Division of Chronic Diseases, the first operating unit in the US Public Health Service to be concerned exclusively with health of 45+ persons. Finds no adequate gerontology program in 20 states surveyed.

300 Harris, R. (1975). Breaking the barriers to better health care delivery for the aged: Medical aspects. The Gerontologist, 15(1). 52-56.
High-level planning and improved financing called for to combat problems arising from rising medical costs, gaps between Medicare and Medicaid coverage, fragmentation and depersonalization of health and medical services, and multiple chronic health problems among the very old. Training needs emphasized.

301 Himmelstein, D.U.; Woolhandler, S. (1986). Cost without benefit: Administrative waste in US health care. The New England Journal of Medicine, 314(7), 441-445.
Declares that health care delivery involves "astonishingly large" administrative costs of $77 billion yearly for private insurance and public programs, including nursing homes. The Medicare prospective payment system is said to have created a costly Federal enforcement bureaucracy. Argues for a national health plan.

302   Institute of Medicine, Committee on an Aging Society. (1985). Health in an aging society. Washington DC: National Academy Press, 256p.
A comprehensive analysis of essential steps necessary to meet acute and long term care needs of varying sectors of a growing elderly population, together with recommendations for dealing with important research gaps.

303   Lee, P.R. (1980). Health policy issues for the aged: Challenges for the 1980s. Generations, 4(1), 38-40, 73.
Urges closer attention to a fundamental question: whether particular health policy goals and priorities should be national, rather than state or local. Declares that decentralization of Federal policy during the 1970s has created new tensions.

304   Lee, P.R.; Estes, C.L.; LeRoy, L.; Newcomer, R. (1982). Health policy and the aged. Annual Review of Gerontology and Geriatrics, Vol.3, New York: Springer Publishing Company, 361-400.
An excellent survey illustrating "the vulnerability of the aged to capricious and complex Federal and state health and aging policies, as well as broader policy considerations" including cost containment and health program decentralization from Federal to state and local levels.

305   Markson, E.W.; Steel, K.; Kane, E. (1983) Administratively necessary days: More than an administrative problem. The Gerontologist, 23(5) 486-492.
Discharge planners at 49 Massachusetts hospitals were surveyed in 1981. Wide variations in procedures suggest that some hospitals seek transfers to institutions as course of first resort, while others seek in-home linkages. Survey coincided with adoption of Massachusetts prospective payment system (PPS).

306   Marmor, T.R. (1981). National health insurance and an aging society. In: Johnston, P.W. (Ed.) Perspectives on aging: Exploding the myths. Cambridge MA: Ballinger Publishing Co., 9-27.
Assesses three prominent national health insurance proposals and concludes that elderly would be better off than under Medicare and Medicaid. But warns that "medicalization" of services could occur unless care is taken to recognize importance of nonmedical personal care services provided by social service agencies.

307   National Council of Senior Citizens. (1986). For-profit hospital care: Who profits? Who cares? Washington DC: 60p.
Finds higher costs and inferior care in proprietary hospitals as compared to nonprofits. Asserts that Federal policy subsidizes for-profit hospital corporations through equity and depreciation policies, and that physicians are caught in a profit vs. good medical practice conflict.

308   Newman, H.N. (1972) Medicare and Medicaid. The Annals of the American Academy of Political and Social Science. 399(January), 114-124.
Medicare and Medicaid regarded as a new kind of Federal commitment in health care financing, but one that failed to provide for expanded service supply and therefore contributed to health care cost inflation. Health maintenance organizations, or HMOs, seen as a means to promote efficiency.

309   Palmore, E. (1983). Health care needs of the rural elderly. International Journal of Aging and Human Development, 18(1), 39-45.

Rural elders have greater illness, but get less health care than urban elders, analysis of National Center for Health Statistics data reveals. Barriers include ignorance and denial, frequent use of lay rather than professional treatment, financial
and transportation difficulties, and resistance of medical personnel.

310   Phillips, H.T. (1985). National health policies for the elderly. In: Phillips,
      H.T.; Gaylord, S.A. (Eds.). Aging and public health. New York: Springer Pub-
      lishing Company, 293-308.
Examines the roles of government relevant to public health and analyzes the cap-
abilities of present programs to fulfill essential responsibilities. Argues that
integration of services for the elderly is the ideal, but that an interim approach
would make better use of many extant system components.

311   Rosenberg, C.E. (1986). The aged in a structured social context: Medicine as
      a case study. In: Van Tassel, D.; Stearns, P.N. (Eds.). Old age in a bureau-
      cratic society: The elderly, the experts, and the state in American history.
      New York: Greenwood Press, 231-246.
Describes varying ways in which medical care has been made available to the
elderly throughout history of the United States. Current deficiences are related to
over-emphasis on acute care and limited attention to sustained care/support.

312   Schaeffer, L.D. (1979). Making compassionate programs work efficiently.
      Aging, Nos.295-296, 21-24.
Efficient management is viewed by the head of the US Health Care Financing
Administration as an act of compassion unlocking resources for human needs.
Describes growing costs of Medicare and Medicaid and efforts by HCFA to improve
efficiency and eliminate an estimated $1.4 billion in fraud, abuse, and waste.

313   Shanas, E. (1978). New directions in health care for the elderly. In:
      Brookbank, J.W. (Ed.). Improving the quality of health care for the elderly.
      Gainesville FL: University of Florida Center for Gerontological Studies and
      Programs. 1-9.
Examining findings from her 1975 and 1962 Surveys of the Aged, the author finds
that frail aged being taken care of at home outnumber those in institutions two to
one; and, that in 13 years, there had been no major change in the functional
capacity of older persons. She calls for a more balanced health care system.

314   Shanas, E.; Maddox, G.L. (1985). Health, health resources, and the utilization
      of care. In: Binstock, R.H.; Shanas, E. (Eds.). Handbook of aging and the
      social sciences. New York: Van Nostrand Reinhold Company, 696-726.
This authoritative review puts special emphasis on the "mismatch between the
health care needs of older persons and the organization of resources to meet those
needs," primarily through neglect of community-based primary, preventive or reha-
bilitative care. Health and illness as social concerns are emphasized.

315   Somers, A.R. (1981.) The geriatric imperative: A major challenge to the
      health professions. In: Somers, A.R.; Fabian, D.R. (Eds.) The geriatric impera-
      tive: An introduction to gerontology and clinical geriatrics. New York, Apple-
      ton-Century-Crofts, 3-19.
Finds that health care professionals and policymakers have neglected care of
stroke, long term care and third party insurance for such care, patient and family
counseling, and appropriate support for dying patients. A potential "revival of
humanism" is foreseen if the many challenges of geriatrics are heeded.

682 Greene, V.L.; Monahan, D.J. (1984). Comparative utilization of community based long term care services by Hispanic and Anglo elderly in a case management system. Journal of Gerontology, 39(6), 730-735.
In a comprehensive management system in Pima County, Arizona, elderly Hispanic clients tend to be more functionally impaired than Anglo counterparts but still use fewer agency-provided community services. Warns against over-reliance on family and friends.

683 Guttmann, D.; Cuellar, J.B. (1982). Barriers to equitable service. Generations, 6(3), 31-33.
Study findings indicate minority group membership is a significant factor in under- and non-utilization of public benefits. Logistical and psychological factors act as barriers, together with restrictive procedures and administrative policies of service providers. Calls for service delivery on need basis.

684 Holmes, M.; Alfaro, J. (1982). Services to minority elderly: Area agency, service provider, and minority elderly perspectives. Summary report. New York: Community Research Applications, 16p.
A study conducted during 1980-81 included questionnaires to all Older Americans Act area agencies on aging and site visits to 16 agencies in 12 states. One finding was that area agency special efforts for minority elderly, other than outreach, were sparse. Recommendations offered.

685 Jackson, J.J. (1976). Aged blacks: A potpourri in the direction of the reduction of inequities. In: Hess, B.B. (Ed.). Growing old in America. New Brunswick NJ: Transaction Books. 390-416.
Proposes reducing the minimum age-eligibility requirements for Old-Age, Survivors, Disability and Health Insurance (OASDHI, in the Social Security System). Supportive arguments emphasize disparities in life expectancy rates. Work of the National Caucus on the Black Aged discussed.

686 Johnson, R. (1978). Barriers to adequate housing for elderly blacks. Aging, Nos. 287-288, 33-39.
Gaps in US Department of Housing and Urban Development data on the black elderly seen as an important factor in inadequate response to their shelter needs. Major Federal programs discussed; public housing viewed as most important to elderly blacks; HUD prototype models seen as vital.

687 Kamikawa, L.M. (1981). The elderly: A Pacific/Asian perspective. Aging, Nos. 319-320, 2-9.
Emphasizes diversity of Pacific Islanders and Asian Americans, and the generally smaller proportion of their elderly when compared to the general population. Federal and other policymakers urged to act in "a society which has systematically neglected their needs." A call for "creative legislation" is made.

688 Kii, T. (1984). Asians. In: Palmore, E.B. (Ed.). Handbook on the aged in the United States. Westport CT: Greenwood Press. 201-17.
Includes a succinct, useful review of literature reporting under-utilization of available formal support systems by elderly Asian Americans, possibly because of their avoidance of them or possibly because of inadequate outreach by service providers. Recommendations made to the US Administration on Aging.

689 Lacayo, C.G. (1982). Triple jeopardy: Underserved Hispanic elders. Generations, 6(3), 25, 59.
Cites data showing Hispanic elderly to be in great social and economic need, yet
they do not rely heavily on social services or family support. Causes include: lack
of money to pay charges, language barrier, and limited ability of service providers
to deal with influxes of older Hispanics.

690 Lambrinos, J.J.; Torres-Gil, F. (1980). Policymakers historically ignore minorities. Generations, 4(1), 24, 72.
Argues that continued policy analysis of minority problems must include a new
dimension: "that of the universal and overall impact of minority concerns on general public issues." Older Americans Act held an example of a barebones program
under which funding austerity will have special impact upon minorities.

691 Lindsay, I. (1971). The multiple hazards of age and race: The situation of
aged blacks in the United States. Washington DC: US Senate. Special Committee on Aging. S.Report 92-450, 73p.
A summation of difficulties facing "an especially disadvantaged group, particularly
if age is added to other handicaps." Discusses problems related to lifestyle, social
and emotional factors. Offers policy recommendations.

692 Meyers, A.R. (1980). Ethnicity and aging: Public policy and ethnic differences
in aging and old age. In: Markson, E.W.; Batra, G.R. (Eds.). Public policies
for an aging population. Lexington MA: Lexington Books, 61-79.
Recognizes that public policy cannot fashion programs for each ethnic group, but
argues for greater effort to preserve ethnic identity through understanding of
varying cultures and sensitivity in such basic functions as needs assessment: "Ethnicity is more than pasta and soul food: it is a fundamental fact of life."

693 Murdock, S.H.; Schwartz, D.F. (1978). Family structure and the use of agency
services: An examination of patterns among elderly Native Americans. The
Gerontologist, 18(5), 475-481.
Native Americans (N=160) living on a Sioux reservation in the Dakotas were interviewed about perceived service needs. Uniformly high requirements were recorded,
suggesting that service agencies involve younger family members in information
dissemination and actual delivery of services.

694 Newton, F.C. (1980). Issues in research and service delivery among Mexican
American elderly: A concise statement with recommendations. The Gerontologist, 20(2), 208-213.
Questions conflicting findings about service use obtained in an extensive review of
the literature; criticizes researchers' tendency to treat the population as if it
were homogeneous. Author offers suggestions to help policymakers and providers
better weigh vital cultural, demographic, and geographical considerations.

695 Register, J.C. (1981). Aging and race: A black-white comparative analysis.
The Gerontologist, 21(4), 438-443.
Examines 1974 national survey (N=4254) to test hypothesis that young and elderly
blacks have more favorable attitudes toward aging than whites. Finds that black
respondents from ages 18-64 are more positive, but those over age 65 are not.
Policy implications include need for diversified program response.

696   Rogers, C.J.; Gallion, T.E. (1978). Characteristics of elderly Pueblo Indians in New Mexico. The Gerontologist, 18(5), 482-487.
A listing of 60+ elderly individuals in 19 pueblos in provided names of 462 individuals selected for interviews. Majority-culture requirements in many Federal programs found to be disruptive of family, clan, and tribal ties. Suggestions made to improve flexibility, outreach, and tribal involvement.

697   Sheppard, N.A. (1978). A Federal perspective on the black aged: From concern to action. Aging, Nos.287-288, 28-32.
Using studies from the Federal Council on the Aging and other material, a Council deputy urges mechanisms for assuring compliance in equitable access to services and adequate income maintenance. Housing seen as a priority for action. Affirmative action throughout aging network recommended.

698   Torres-Gil, F. (1986). An examination of factors affecting future cohorts of elderly Hispanics. The Gerontologist, 26(2), 140-146.
Hispanics' recent strides in improved educational levels expected to be a factor helping the next two generations "make their need heard, to advocate and lobby, and to negotiate the maze of public benefits and public bureaucracies." But the author's examination of civil rights protection points to shortcomings.

699   Torres-Gil, F. (1986). Hispanics: a special challenge. In: Pifer, A.; Bronte, L. (Eds.). Our aging society: Paradox and promise. New York: W.W. Norton, 219-242.
Possible policy conflicts may emerge as Hispanics mature in an aging society. Raising of Social Security eligibility to 67 after year 2022 will have unique consequences; possible development of a two-tier health care system more rigorously dividing the well-off and low-income would also have special impact.

700   Torres-Gil, F. (1982). Politics of aging among elder Hispanics. Washington DC: University Press of America. 211p.
At a time when Federal and State governments have begun to recognize the diversity of elderly Hispanics and have responded with more responsive public programming, the "New Federalism" philosophy could cause disappearance of some gains. Future directions discussed. Bibliography.

701   Torres-Gil, F.; Negm, M. (1980). Policy issues concerning the Hispanic elderly. Aging, Nos.305-306, 2-5.
Questions effectiveness of Federal policies for minority elders. Negative factors include census undercounting, failure to recognize and respond to cultural factors, differences in eligibility for services, information gaps, lack of minority representation, and discrimination.

702   US Commission on Civil Rights. (1982). Minority elderly services: New programs, old problems. 163p, Pt.I; 125p, Pt.II.
A six-city survey, together with staff interviews and questionnaires, results in findings that the US Administration on Aging and the Older Americans Act state and area agencies follow staffing and service delivery policies adversely affecting minorities. Commission recommends clarifying legislation.

703   Watson, W.H. (1986). Crystal ball gazing: Notes on today's middle aged blacks with implications for their aging in the 21st Century. The Gerontologist, 26(2), 136-139.
Clustering of blacks in selected, peripheral occupations persists despite civil rights and affirmative action breakthroughs, contributing to comparative decline in black family income. Gains foreseen as minor in coming decades. Author calls for radical improvement in enforcing antidiscrimination laws.

704   Wershow, H.J. (1976). Inadequate census data on black nursing home patients. The Gerontologist, 16(1), 86-87.
An investigation of nursing home patients in Alabama leads author to criticize poor census reporting on black patients and black nursing homes. Examples from other states provided to document "massive undercounting of black nursing home patients." A plea for better Federal statistics is made.

RESEARCH

705   Benedict, R.C. (1980). The TG Interview: Robert Benedict, US Commissioner, Administration on Aging. The Gerontologist, 20(2), 131-139.
Priorities and procedures for research grants through the Older Americans Act dominate this interview. Frank responses from the Commissioner illuminate the problems faced by an agency with modest funding and staff shortages. Working relationships with university gerontology centers, Congressional attitudes, discussed.

706   Birren, J.E. (1968). Research on aging: A frontier of science and social gain. The Gerontologist, 8(1), 7-13.
Urges "an adequate national source of fundamental knowledge on which future services and sound administration of programs can be based." Calls for Federally-assisted university-based research institutes, personnel training, and special emphasis on health screening and promotion.

707   Bixby, L.E.; Ireland, L.M. (1969). The Social Security Administration program of retirement research. The Gerontologist, 9(2), 143-147.
Briefly traces SSA studies that began within a year after first Social Security payments were made in 1940. Retirement History Study begun in 1968 is of special interest as the first longitudinal survey undertaken by SSA. An objective, informative account of special interest for its emphasis on key policy issues.

708   Butler, R.N. (1980). The alliance of advocacy with science. The Gerontologist, 20(2), 154-162.
Declares that a fourth and separate power of government (other than law-making, law-enforcing, and law-interpreting) should be "the knowledge-base providing function." Author's experience at the National Institute on Aging has impressed him by the "ramshackle, haphazard way in which health science policy is often made."

709   Butler, R.N. (1976). Early directions for the National Institute on Aging (Editorial). The Gerontologist, 16(4), 293-4.
Recognizing the need for biologic research and training, the new NIA director promises "greater program balance in order to support new efforts in medicine and the social and psychological sciences," as well as innovative health and other service delivery. Research personnel training goals given.

710   Butler, R.N. (1976). To find the answers. In: Gross, R.; Gross, B.; Seidman, S. The new old: Struggling for decent aging. Garden City NY: Anchor Books. 241-49.
"Research is the ultimate service, and the ultimate cost container," asserts the author soon after his appointment as director of the National Institute on Aging. Gives examples of basic research value; describes relationships to other research fields. Reports on plans to work with other Federal agencies.

711   Cassell, C.K. (1985). Ethical issues in research in geriatrics. In: Moody, H.R. (Ed.). Ethics and aging. Generations, 9(2), 45-48.
Summarizes principles from Federal studies on biomedical research involving the elderly, relating general principles to specific, difficult issues arising in nursing homes and other sites chosen for research. Provides suggested topics for research needed "to further understanding of ethical research in geriatrics."

712   Cohen, E.S. (1970). Research and public policy: Relevance for decisionmaking. The Gerontologist, 10(3), 198-201.
Offers recommendations for increasing utilization of research findings in public policy decisions, emphasizing need for new relationships by universities and operating agencies for maximum interaction.

713   Cornman, J.M. (1986). Statistical policy for an aging America. Statement at a hearing of the US Senate Committee on Governmental Affairs, Subcommittee on Governmental Processes, June 3. 12p.

Testimony by the Executive Director of the Gerontological Society of America focuses on protection and improvement of data bases "on which sound public policies and many private decisions rest." Summarizes previous GSA findings; makes recommendations.

714   Freeman, J.T. (1980). Some notes on the history of the National Institute on Aging. The Gerontologist, 20(5), 610-614.
An informative account of growing Federal involvement in gerontological research, beginning with establishment of a unit on aging in the Division of Chemotherapy at the National Institutes of Health in July 1940.   Other steps leading to authorization of the National Institute on Aging in 1974 described.

715   Lebowitz, B.D. (1981). Funding agencies and the research community. The Gerontologist, 21(4), 382-387.
Setting of research agendas is seen as a priority goal, perhaps performed by an independent body or commission. Independence of scientists can be enhanced by "a diversity of approach to a common core of issues." Translation of research into action is often neglected but can be broadened.

716   Lebowitz, B.D. (1979). The management of research in aging: A case study in science policy. The Gerontologist, 19(2), 151-162.
Examines seven Administration on Aging-funded studies on the coordination of services. This "directed research" is found to have generated "high-quality, useful information." Further discussion seen as necessary on preserving scientific independence in other kinds of research.

717   Newcomer, R.J.; Estes, C.L.; Freeman, H.E. (1985). Strategies of research for program design and intervention. In: Binstock, R.H.; Shanas, E. (Eds.). Handbook of aging and the social sciences. New York: Van Nostrand Reinhold Company, 619-640.
Assumes that social science research can and does produce results with policy and program relevance; provides incisive commentary on models and hypotheses. Relates its conceptual approach to actual policy challenges and argues for greater focus in delineation and more thoroughness in investigating policy options.

718   Storey, J.R. (1984). Recent changes in the availability of Federal data on the aged. Washington DC: Gerontological Society of America, 50p.
1980s described as difficult years for those concerned with Federal data collection and research related to aging. Documents delays, abandonments, or reductions in important Federal surveys.

719   US National Institute on Aging. (1982). Toward an independent old age: A national plan for research on aging. NIH Pub.82-2453, GPO 0-388-904/BID, 361p.
Intended to help develop "a long-range plan for promoting health and well-being by extending the vigorous and productive years of life through research on aging." Findings developed by study panels deal with aging processes, clinical manifestations of age-related disorders, and older people and a dynamic society.

720   US National Institute on Aging. (1977). Our future selves: A research plan toward understanding aging. DHEW Pub. 77-1096, 60p.
An initial plan, prepared by NIA with the assistance of the National Advisory Council on Aging, responding to a 1974 Congressional mandate to develop a program coordinating research in the biological, medical, psychological, social, educational, and economic aspects of aging.

721   US Senate. Special Committee on Aging. (1971). Research and training needs in gerontology. Committee Print, 73p.
Papers by Gerontological Society leaders discuss biomedical aspects, medical education, medical care research, ways to meet research and training needs, and needed social research. Establishment of a national aging institute is a major recommendation.

722   Wales, J.B.; Treybig, D.L. (1978). Recent legislative trends toward the protection of human subjects: Implications for gerontologists. The Gerontologist, 18(3), 244-249.
Raises the issue of whether special risk on the basis of advanced age should be a factor in protection afforded to human subjects in biomedical and behavioral research, and invites additional discussion. Reviews legislation providing such protection to identified risk groups.

RURAL PROGRAMS

723   Ambrosius, G.R. (1982). Overcoming underservice in rural America. Generations, 6(3). 40-41.
Barriers to effective Federal action are listed as restrictive regulatory language, an urban bureaucracy, insensitive urban delivery models, limited management expertise, and low priority to generation of local resources. Urges local initiatives, greater program flexibility.

724   Beall, G.T.; Thompson, M.M.; Goodwin, F.; Donahue, W.T. (1981). Housing
        older persons in rural America: A handbook on congregate housing. Wash-
        ington DC: International Center for Social Gerontology, 259p.
Chapter I provides informative background on congregate housing on the rural
milieu, relating a US Farmers Home Administration demonstration program to
essential principles of rurality and assisted independent living. Useful bibliography,
references, appendices.

725   Coward, R.T. (1979). Planning community services for the rural elderly:
        implications from research. The Gerontologist, 19(3), 275-282.
This broadbased review of research on rural elderly emphasizes rural diversity and
identifies key elements needed to develop new strategies. Article is directed at
practitioners, but has policy ramifications.

726   Krout, J.A. (1986). The aged in rural America. Westport CT: Greenwood
        Press, 182p.
Valuable summary of research and statements compiled by author for earlier bibliography, together with new, detailed rationale for his argument that "little if any
effort has been made at the Federal level to develop a viable policy to address
unique problems of the rural elderly." Special focus on the Older Americans Act.

727   Krout, J.A. (1983). Correlates of service utilization among the rural elderly.
        The Gerontologist, 23(5), 500-504.
Interviews (N=5,700) in a New York non-metropolitan county finds that rates of
service knowledge and utilization were generally comparable to those reported for
the metropolitan aged. Over 70 percent of the sample had not heard of an information and referral service.

728   McGhee, J.L. (1983). Transportation opportunity and the rural elderly: A com-
        parison of objective and subjective indicators. The Gerontologist, 23(5),
        505-511.
Interviews (N=231) in an Indiana county led to findings of economic, physicial and
social characteristics of "transportation dependents," comprising 43.3 percent of
the sample. Women found to be most disadvantaged.

729   Nofz, M.P. (1986). Social services for older rural Americans: Some policy
        concerns. Social Work, 31(2), 85-91.
Calls for regionally focused research, service delivery to accommodate varying
rural needs and to correct maldistribution of Federal resources. Excellent references.

730   Pressler, L. (1984). Rural and small-city elderly. US Senate. Special Commit-
        tee on Aging, SuDoc Y4.Ag4:Sprt.98-223, 11p.
A Senator from South Dakota gives reasons for concluding that "the rural elderly
are not receiving their just share of the support and assistance available." Evaluates health, housing, nutrition programs and the Older Americans Act. Findings
based partially on survey of state aging agencies.

731   Sutherland, D.E. (1983). Rural elderly confronted by special circumstances.
        Perspective on Aging, 12(3), 11-13.
To counter "a subtle but systematic pattern of discrimination in funding for rural
areas," author sees need for specialized training of personnel, a 7-issue research
effort recognizing rural values, and clearcut links between training and research.

TRAINING

732   Anderson, T.E.; Blank, M.L. (1970). Education and training in gerontology—
        1970: National Institute of Mental Health. The Gerontologist, 10(2), 153-55.
Gives brief history of NIMH objectives in training of mental health personnel, first
begun in 1948; describes NIMH aging-related grants in 1970 ranging from social
work courses to geropsychiatry and continuing education for mental health agency
staff members. Followed by 5 pages giving 24 examples of university projects.

733   Duncan, L.E. (1970). National Institute of Child Health and Human Develop-
        ment training grant programs. The Gerontologist, 10(1), p.62.
NICHD support for training of aging, begun in 1964 with a total of $194,000 and
increased to $2.3 million by 1969, is described by the Institute Director in an
interesting account of pre-National Institute on Aging activities and goals.
Followed by list of grants and 23 examples of university programs on six pages.

734   Flint, H.M. (1970). Training in social gerontology. In: Hoffman, A.M. (Ed.) The
        daily needs and interests of older people. Springfield IL: Charles C. Thomas,
        427-448.
Informative review of gerontological training needs and Federal programs available
at the time, including those offered by the National Institutes of Health, the
National Institute of Mental Health, and other units within the Department of
Health, Education, and Welfare.

735   Institute of Medicine. (1978). Aging and medical education. Washington DC:
        National Academy of Sciences, IOM Pub. 78-04, 64p.
Finds that undergraduate medical education does not provide adequate exposure to
many medical problems graduates will face, particularly in continuing care of
patients with multiple, chronic, interacting disabilities. Recommends improvement in
medical school curricula and practices.

736   Mather, J.H.; Dube, W.F. (1981). Veterans Administration's development of
        health professionals education programs in geriatrics and gerontology. In:
        Somers, A.R.; Fabian, D.R. (Eds.) The geriatric imperative: An introduction to
        gerontology and clinical geriatrics. New York, Appleton–Century–Crofts,
        329-35.
Faced by sharp increases in the number of elderly veterans, the VA has developed
a plan to prepare trained health care providers in geriatric medicine and gerontology. Legislative mandates posed in the Veterans Omnibus Health Care Act of
1976 discussed.

737   Surveys and Research Corporation. (1969). The demand for personnel and
        training in the field of aging. Washington DC: Administration on Aging Pub.
        270, 201p.
A study ordered by a 1967 Federal statute finds a major shortage of trained and
specialized personnel in aging. Management personnel for retirement housing, recreation, and long term care facilities expected to rise from 45,000 in 1969 to
84,000 by 1970 and 105,000 trained persons by 1980.

738   Tibbitts, C.L. (1970). Administration on Aging's Title V training grant pro-
        gram. The Gerontologist, 10(1), 54-56.

An informative account by a leader in social gerontology, then chief of the AoA Training Grants staff, giving reasons for policies and priorities adopted after the AoA Title V training grants program became operational in January 1966. Sees a need for increased support for long- and short-term training.

739   US Public Health Service. (1984). Report on education and training in geriatrics and gerontology. Administrative Document. 98p.
Identifies deficiencies in Federal programs conducted by Administration on Aging, Health Resources and Services Administration, National Institute on Aging, and National Institute of Mental Health. Offers a plan to improve and extend such efforts.

740   US Veterans Administration. (1985). The Geriatric Research, Education, and Clinical Centers: GRECC. VA Pub. IBI8-4, 32p.
Describes centers established in 1975 to attract outstanding professionals to teach and to conduct research in a clinical context. Details given for 10 GRECCs located at VA Medical Centers, and for Interdisciplinary Team Training in Geriatrics (ITTG).

WOMEN

741   Block, M.R. (Ed.). (1982). The direction of Federal legislation affecting women over forty. College Park MD: National Policy Center on Women and Aging, University of Maryland, 162p.
A compilation of Federal legislation over 50 years, identifying inequities to women that often appear in "male model" programs. Authors deal with health care, mental health, employment and training, education, income maintenance, housing, transportation, energy, and crime victimization. Lengthy bibliography.

742   Hess, B.B. (1980). Old women: Problems, potentials, and policy implications. In: Markson, E.W.; Batra, G.R. (Eds.). Public policies for an aging population. Lexington MA: Lexington Books, 39-59.
Identifies shortcomings of Social Security and other programs in assisting women, not only homemakers but working women. Advises that public policy should have two foci, the dependent and independent: "Programs that encourage the latter should eventually reduce the former." Numerous notes.

743   Hess, B.B. (1986). Antidiscrimination policies today and the life chances of older women tomorrow. The Gerontologist, 26(2), 132-35.
An examination of shortcomings in antidiscrimination legislation, as compounded by the probable dilution of recent women's occupational gains because of elimination of many traditional job niches. "Earnings sharing" to improve Social Security treatment of women, together with pay equity, seen essential.

744   Kahne, H. (1985). Not yet equal: Employment experience of older women and older men. International Journal of Aging and Human Development. 22(1), 1-13.
Women aged 45 and over make up almost 30 percent of the female civilian labor force and 40 percent of the older labor force. They are disadvantaged in six ways. An "effective Federal affirmative action policy" including better employment counseling and assistance is proposed.

745   Markson, E.W. (1984). Family roles and the impact of feminism on women's
       mental health. In: Hess, B.B.; Sussman, M.B. (Eds.). Women and the family:
       Two decades of change. New York: Haworth Press. 215-232.
A brief discussion of women 65-years old and over describes them as most disadvantaged women's age group of all, not helped much by positive judicial and
legislative changes affecting women in general. Many references.

746   Minkler, M.; Stone, R. (1985). The feminization of poverty and older women.
       The Gerontologist, 25(4), 351-357.
Elderly women's poverty rate of 19 percent described as highest for any United
States age group; 1980 census showed half of all older women had annual incomes
below $5,000. Health expenditures are higher than men's. Budget cuts and new
workforce trends could worsen older women's situation.

747   Muller, C. (1983). Income supports for older women. Social Policy, 14(2),
       23-31.
Takes a broad perspective recognizing "the interplay of historical, attitudinal,
labor market, and legislative factors in determining the needs and resources of women as they face their later years of life." Policy recommendations call for
immediate and long-range changes.

748   University of Michigan. Institute of Gerontology. (1984). Women, work and
       age: Policy challenges. Ann Arbor MI, 26p.
Status of older worker women and their opportunities for fair and equal access to
rewarding employment or job training discussed in conference proceedings summary.
Articles emphasize age/sex discrimination, poverty pitfalls, minority problems,
fringe benefits, and occupational safety. Well-organized bibliography.

749   US Senate. Special Committee on Aging Task Force. (1975). Women and Social
       Security: Adapting to a new era. SuDoc Y4.Ag4:W84, 87p.
A distinguished Task Force (Dorothy McCamman, Chairperson) summarizes women's
Social Security difficulties, many of them arising from "pervasive injustice to
women in the job market." Pro and con arguments given for 16 potential recommendations; Task Force then gives its proposals.

750   US Public Health Service. Task Force On Women's Health Issues. (1985).
       Health concerns of older women. Public Health Reports. 100(1). 92-95.
An excerpt from Vol.I of the Task Force report, this summary catalogues physical
health concerns including osteoporosis and dietary habits, mental health issues, and
drug misuse and abuse. Its "key to good health" is a "combination of successful
health promotion efforts throughout life and adequate access to health care."

751   Warlick, J.L. (1985). Why is poverty after 65 a woman's problem? Journal of
       Gerontology, 40(6), 751-757.
Two of every three poor elderly persons are women. Problems arising during work
histories include less access to market incomes. Changes in Social Security proposed; limited effects of the 1984 Retirement Equity Act discussed.

APPENDIX

SOURCES OF INFORMATION:
CONGRESSIONAL COMMITTEES
AND NATIONAL ORGANIZATIONS

CONGRESSIONAL COMMITTEES

As noted in the preface, citations in this bibliography to Congressional publications are limited to reports issued by Committees. They do not include published hearings, which usually contain informative statements by expert witnesses on complex issues, as well as useful statistical and background data. Frequently, testimony by older persons and their family members gives a human dimension to such proceedings.

Monthly abstracts published by the Congressional Information Service provide convenient summaries of major points made at hearings, together with names of all witnesses. The Monthly Catalogue of United States Government Publications lists published hearings, but offers little information about content.

The US Senate Special Committee on Aging (G-33 Dirksen Building, Washington DC 20510) gives brief summaries of hearings for the prior year in its annual report, Developments in Aging. In addition, each issue of Developments lists all publications issued by the Committee since its founding in 1961. Overall, the Committee's annual report is a useful summation of legislative actions, as well as a rich source of background material on policy matters. Part II of Developments is devoted to reports from Federal departments and agencies on their activities related to aging.

The US House of Representatives Select Committee on Aging (House Annex One, Room 712, Washington DC 20515) has, since its establishment in 1974, published many hearing transcripts and reports. A Committee Publications List, available on request, gives information about the availability of each of them. In October 1986, the Committee issued: "Legislative Highlights-99th Congress. A Brief Review of Legislation of Interest to Older Americans."

NATIONAL ORGANIZATIONS

Compendiums of legislative objectives are issued by a number of national organizations on aging. They are advocacy-oriented, but often give substantial data, historical background on programs, and accounts of current difficulties or achievements of public policy.

The American Association of Retired Persons (1909 K Street NW, Washington DC 20049) compiles an annual, book-length report on legislative objectives and the rationales for each. Limited numbers are available to serious researchers. An abbreviated version is also issued.

The National Council on the Aging (600 Maryland Avenue SW, West Wing 100, Washington DC 20024) publishes a biennial public policy agenda in its magazine, Perspective on Aging. NCOA's entire March/April 1986 issue of Perspective was devoted to the 1986-1987 agenda.

The National Council of Senior Citizens (925 15th Street NW, Washington DC 20005) compiles an annual legislative program and includes it as an insert in the spring edition of its monthly Senior Citizens News. Reprints are available. NCSC also publishes a year-end legislative summary, as well as occasional bulletins.

The Gerontological Society of America (1411 K Street NW, Suite 300, Washington DC, 20005) focuses on Federal policy related to research and training. In 1986, GSA issued a publication summing up policy and other issues arising from an upsurge of interest in intergenerational tensions. (See entry 669)

The American Society on Aging (formerly the Western Gerontological Society, 833 Market Street, Room 516, San Francisco CA 94103), in its bimonthly Connection, often publishes "Focus" sections dealing with public affairs. ASA's quarterly journal, Generations, devotes each issue to one subject, frequently with extensive attention to policy matters.

The Gray Panthers (311 South Juniper Street, Suite 601, Philadelphia PA 19107) comment on a wide range of policy issues in their bimonthly tabloid, Gray Panther Network: Age and Youth in Action. The organization also issues a monthly Health Watch.

The Villers Advocacy Associates (1334 G Street NW, Washington DC 20005) cooperates with other organizations to distribute ASAP: Advocates Senior Alert Process to provide current information on legislative issues. The Villers Foundation (same address), in January 1987 published a book, On the Other Side of Easy Street: Myths and Facts About the Economics of Old Age, intended to combat characterizations of older Americans as greedy and unworthy of governmental support.

More specialized information is provided by other organizations.

The National Association of State Units on Aging and the National Association of Area Agencies on Aging (both at 600 Maryland Avenue SW, Suite 208 West, Washington DC 20024) compile information on program operations under the Older Americans Act. Their National Data Base on Aging also gives details about state and area agencies on aging.

Publications of the American Association of Homes for the Aged (1129 20th Street, Suite 400, Washington DC 20036) are useful for information on housing programs as well as long term care legislation.

The Older Women's League (1325 G Street NW, Lower Lobby B, Washington DC 20005) often relates its concerns to broad policy issues.

Among the other organizations providing information on specific policy matters are:

AFL-CIO Department of Occupational Safety, Health, and Social Security, 815 16th Street NW, Washington DC 20006.

American Association for International Aging, 1511 K Street NW, Suite 1028, Washington DC 20036.

American Bar Association Commission on Legal Problems of the Elderly, 1800 M Street NW, Washington DC 20036.

American Health Care Association (formerly the American Nursing Home Association), 1200 15th Street NW, Washington DC 20005.

American Psychiatric Association (Council on Aging), 1400 K Street NW, Washington DC 20005.

American Psychological Association, 1200 17th Street NW, Washington DC 20036.

American Public Health Association (Gerontological Health Section), 1015 15th Street NW, Washington DC 20005.

Asociacion Nacional Pro Personas Mayores, 2727 West 6th Street, Suite 270, Los Angeles CA 90057.

Association for Gerontology in Higher Education, 6700 Maryland Avenue SW, Suite 204 West, Washington DC 20024.

National Association for Home Care, 519 C Street NE, Washington DC 20002.

National Association of Counties, 440 First Street NW, Washington DC 20001.

National Caucus and Center on Black Aged, 1424 K Street NW, Suite 500, Washington DC 20005.

National Citizens' Coalition for Nursing Home Reform, 1424 16th Street NW, Suite L2, Washington DC 20036.

National Indian Council on Aging, P.O. Box 2088, Albuquerque, NM 87103.

National Pacific/Asian Resource Center on Aging, 1341 G Street NW, Suite 311, Washington DC 20005.

National Senior Citizens Law Center, 2025 M Street NW, Suite 400, Washington DC 20036.

Pension Rights Center 1701 K Street, Suite 305, Washington DC 20006.

US Conference of Mayors (Aging Program), 1620 Eye Street NW, Washington DC 20006.

AUTHOR INDEX

SUBJECT INDEX

Factors in Development, 009,015,
    062,077,113,133
Historical Perspective, 001,002,
    019,027,028,031,032,033,045,
    051,056,074,076,083,090,096,
    111,115,116,122,126,134,139,
    153,154,155,156,161,286
Legal Issues, 003,026,086,098,159
Measuring Economic Hardship, 029
Need for Outreach, 141
Need for Re-Examination, 006,012,
    013,017,036,037,038,043,052,
    058,060,063,064,082,089,091,
    100,101,109,110,114,118,124
    134,147,158,160,162
"Old Age Policy System", 116
Presidential Messages, 068,071,
    072,108
Public Support for, 024,030,055,
    078,131
Revenue Sharing, 070
Segregates Elderly, 043,125
State Role in, 028,081
The "New Ageism", 069
The Elderly Poor, 092
White House Conferences, 004,033,
    057,067,075,085,097,099,144,
    145,146,149,152

HEALTH CARE ETHICAL ISSUES
282,283,284,285

HEALTH CARE STRUCTURE
Competition Impact, 295
Deficiencies in, 036,107,288,290,
    291,294,300,302,304,310,311,
    312,313,314,315,318
Elderly Advocacy, 293
Federal Role, 286,289,298,299,317
Future Demands on, 048,292,303,615
Future Service Needs, 319
Health Maintenance Organizations,
    287,296,308,445,446
Hospice Role, 297
Hospital Backup, 305,307
Information Technology, 316
"Medicalization", 110,320
National Health Plan, 301,306,437
Rural Needs, 309

HEALTH PROMOTION
299,316,321,322,323,324,325,326,
327,706

HOME HEALTH SERVICES
Conflicting Policies, 328,329,
    331,333,336,337,338,339,341,
    342,385
Cost Containment, 343
Cost Savings, 334,340,421
Federal Role, 298
Grant Program, 335
Massachusetts Program, 334,354
New York Home Care, 352
Rural, 330,332

HOUSING
Age as Eligibility Criterion,
    532,554
And Minorities, 686
Capital Gains Policy, 546
Congregate, 525,529,534,536,541
    724
Cooperative, 523
Cutbacks, 559,563
Deinstitutionalization, 477
Essential Role of, 158,524,531,
    542,545
For Impaired Elderly, 382,402,532
Future Needs, 522,535,548,551,556,
    557,558,560
Home Equity, 561
Home Repair, 539
Housing Impact, 537,553
"Overhoused" Elderly, 530,555
Relocation, 550
Research, 527,533
Rural, 543,724
Segregation of Elderly, 528
Service Needs, 534,536
Shared Housing, 538,540,552
Single Room Occupancy, 526,562
Suitability for In-Home Services,
    547
Targeting Strategies, 522,549
Urban Renovation, 544
202 Program Cost Containment, 559

INTERGENERATIONAL CONCERNS
034,101,112,114,192,284,654,660,
    669,670,671,672,673

LEGAL SERVICES
Guardianship, 003,568
Importance, 569
Protective Services, 570,571

About the Compiler

WILLIAM E. ORIOL, currently an author and researcher on aging, is Past Staff Director of the U.S. Senate Special Committee on Aging and Past Associate Director of the International Center for Social Gerontology. He is author of *Getting the Story on Aging, A Sourcebook on Gerontology for Journalists* and *Housing the Elderly Deinstitutionalized Mental Hospital Patient in the Community, The Complex Cube of Long-Term Care*, and *Aging in All Nations*. He has contributed articles to *The Gerontologist, Social Policy*, and the American Society on Aging's *Connection*.